Additional Praise for *Critical Selling*

"As the sales landscape has evolved, so too have the needs of our customers. The methods, research, and strategies provided in this book have given our sales organization the tools they need in today's market to create a positive customer experience, grow relationships, and improve conversion rates. If you are looking to increase sales, I would recommend this book to any salesperson, sales manager, or executive!"

—Brad Hice,
Manager Sales & Finance Programs/Training
Daimler Trucks Remarketing Corp.

"Justin Zappulla and Janek Performance Group have been Santander Bank partners for years. Our Corporate Banking senior sales team was trained on the Critical Selling program and it immediately drove real results. The contents in this book have been able to deliver that special 'click' to our team here at Santander Bank in a recurrent basis which is something unique in a time of 'broad brush approach.'"

—Xavi Ruiz Sena,
Executive Vice President, Head of Finance
Santander Bank

critical selling

How Top Performers **Accelerate** the Sales Process and **Close** More Deals

NICK KANE | JUSTIN ZAPPULLA

WILEY

Published by John Wiley & Sons, Inc., Hoboken, New Jersey.
Published simultaneously in Canada.

For general information on our other products and services or for technical support, please contact our Customer Care Department within the United States at (800) 762–2974, outside the United States at (317) 572–3993 or fax (317) 572–4002.

Wiley also publishes its books in a variety of electronic formats. Some content that appears in print may not be available in electronic books. For more information about Wiley products, visit our website at www.wiley.com.

Library of Congress Cataloging-in-Publication Data:

Kane, Nick.
    Critical selling : how top performers accelerate the sales process and close more deals / Nick Kane, Justin Zappulla.
        pages cm
    Includes index.
    ISBN 978-1-119-05255-5 (cloth); ISBN 978-1-119-05257-9 (ebk); ISBN 978-1-119-05258-6 (ebk)
    1. Selling. 2. Sales management. I. Title.
    HF5438.25.Z37 2016
    658.85–dc23

                                                                                    2015020838

Printed in the United States of America

10 9 8 7 6 5 4 3 2 1

To my beautiful wife, Megan. My true partner in life.
Your love, understanding, encouragement, and unwavering
support are what make everything work. I love you.
And to my brilliant daughters, Alaina and Aubrey.
Always remember the three things . . .
And lastly, to the memory of my grandpa, Richard Zappulla, who
inspired me to work hard, be kind, and always believe in myself.
Thank you. I am forever grateful.

—Justin Zappulla

To my amazing daughters, Alyssa, Emily, and Sophia,
I dedicate this book to you. Your smiles, courage, and enthusiasm
keep me motivated every day! Without your unconditional love
and support, this book would not have been possible.
Remember what I've told you since you were born:
You are destined to do great things in this life!

—Nick Kane

Contents

Acknowledgments

WRITING A BOOK is no small feat. It requires time, dedication, drive, and focus. The motivation for Critical Selling came from our desire to provide real, tangible skills, and best practices to all sales professionals who want to improve their performance in today's selling environment. This book was a team effort and there are many people we would like to acknowledge for their support, guidance, and hard work.

First, we would like to express our sincere gratitude to the best team in the sales performance business, our colleagues at Janek Performance Group. Dana, Rudy, Amy, Mindy, Jerry, Brandon, and the rest of the team. Your unwavering commitment to supporting our clients in achieving their sales objectives is second to none.

Next, we would like to thank our confidant and "Chief Book Officer," Kelli. Your work is truly first class and your zeal, expertise, and insight were paramount in bringing this book to life. We can't thank you enough for the countless hours you invested with us over this past year!

It's important to acknowledge the outstanding publishing team at John Wiley & Sons. A big "high five" to Lia, Shannon, Deborah, Peter, John, Liz, and the rest of the team. Thank you for your patience while guiding a few rookie authors through this process. All of you are true professionals!

Finally, we would like to acknowledge our first true sales family; thanks for giving two young kids an opportunity to be part of and help build a powerhouse sales organization. There is no question; the company changed the lives of thousands of sales professionals both in the United States and abroad, including ours. There was never a dull moment working side by side with who today remain some of our closest friends. Thank you to our personal mentors, Adam, Marty, and Mike. Your leadership and passion for sales excellence still live in us today!

■ ■ ■

Nick would like to personally acknowledge:

I would also like to acknowledge other people who contributed to this book. To my mother, Helen, and father, Mark, thank you for your wisdom, kindness, and courage. To my brother, Eric, and lifelong friend, Aviv, thank you for always being there for me when I needed you the most. To Brittany, thank you for your unconditional love, support, and all that you do. To my family in San Diego, Mila, Mike, Alex, Cindy, and Stella, thank you all for your kindness and encouragement.

Justin would like to personally acknowledge:

I would like to acknowledge the love and support of my family and those closest to me. I cannot thank you all enough for the steady and positive influence you've given me throughout my life, and this book would not be possible without you. Thank you to my mother, Debbie; my sisters, Alisha and Breanna; my Granny, Audrey; my uncle, Joe; my aunts, Rhonda and Carol; Jeff, Bob, Barbara, and Mark. I love you all!

Introduction
Critical Selling: Focusing on What Matters Most

IN A DAY and age when meeting or exceeding quarterly expectations is more important than ever before, it's no secret that companies are constantly looking for ways to improve sales performance. That's because sales are the lifeblood of any company, and so the importance of focusing on sales performance remains a top priority with everyone throughout the organization, from the C-Suite to middle management to sales professionals working in the trenches every day.

In order to survive in today's fiercely competitive global marketplace, it's critical to operate a high-performing sales organization that can outsell the competition. To do this, there is quite a lot to get right, including:

- The right sales strategy
- A compelling value proposition
- A well-defined sales process
- The right sales talent
- Effective sales tools

1

All of these things are crucial if an organization intends to keep firing on all cylinders. But where the rubber really meets the road in sales is in the real-world interactions between the sales professional and the customer.

The fact is that people still buy from people. Sales strategies, process maps, and clear value propositions are all important. But in the end, how each sales professional performs during the critical moments he has with his customers determines whether the deal is closed and the sale is won. It all comes down to execution.

Top sales professionals are always thinking about how they can better execute each and every sales interaction. They take the time to think about the most effective approach they can use with each of their customers. They keep abreast of the skills, best practices, and processes that produce the greatest possible results. And they look for strategic, concrete ways to improve their sales performance.

The Critical Selling framework we'll share with you in these pages is a proven, real-world approach that helps salespeople from all walks of life—any industry, any size company—flawlessly execute sales calls with customers in order to accelerate the sales process and close more deals. We've spent more than a decade conducting ongoing research and identifying best practices in order to develop world-class sales professionals. Our research has focused on two key areas: sellers and buyers. On the selling side, we have worked side by side with hundreds of sales organizations and thousands of salespeople to understand what it is that top-performing sales professionals do (and do better) that other reps don't to win more sales. On the buying side, we've taken a deep look at customers, examining how they investigate and evaluate products and services and how they ultimately make their purchasing decisions. The results we've uncovered have informed the approach outlined in this book.

As such, we know that this is an approach that succeeds in the real world. Following the skills, strategies, and best practices shared in these pages will help ensure that you are fully prepared to accelerate the sales process and close more deals.

One of the most apparent findings from the research we've conducted is that buyers are changing. Today's buyers:

- Are more educated about products and services, and about the selling cycle
- Conduct thorough research into product and service options—before ever connecting with a sales professional
- Bring higher expectations to the selling cycle
- Are becoming increasingly intolerant toward sales reps who resort to aggressive sales tactics
- Do not want to hear a "pitch" in lieu of a tailored solution
- Want sales professionals to bring valuable insights, ideas, and advice to the sales conversation
- Place a greater premium on time
- Have easy access to more alternatives and options

These important changes in customer behavior mean that sales professionals, too, must change. Today's top-performing sales professionals must adapt to busier, smarter, savvier customers, who come to the table with more demands and higher expectations. Those salespeople who embrace this changing landscape by fine-tuning their sales approach using the Critical Selling framework will achieve bigger, better, and more impressive results that bring more value to their customers and to their own organizations.

In the chapters to come, we'll look at specific strategies, skills, and best practices that, when fully embraced, will help today's sales professionals keep pace with tomorrow's customers. We'll also look at how to deal with common missteps. By embracing the approach found in these pages, you will learn how to:

- Accelerate the sales process by quickly discovering what is most important to the customer
- Create solid connections with customers and establish trust using effective relationship-building best practices

- Differentiate yourself from the competition by adding value, insight, and advice to the sales discussion
- Reduce the number of objections and effectively handle those you do receive, along with pushback from customers—at every stage of the process
- Close more deals by adopting a proven, research-based sales approach

Of course, you can't accelerate the sales process and close more deals if you're not building strong relationships with your customers. The fact remains that good sales is all about building good relationships. That happens if—and only if—you're able to establish credibility with your customers. Top performers are much more than order takers with a bright smile and a firm handshake. They're more than merely effective sales professionals. While they can recite product info, values, and benefits as well as—or even better than—anyone else, they know how to go much deeper in order to understand customer needs and to explain how their product or service is in alignment with those needs. They build credibility with their customers. They build relationships. In doing so, they become trusted advisers who know how to sell to today's customers.

Selling to customers well be more challenging than ever before. At a time when customers are better informed than in years past, they've more than likely done a lot of research before they've even thought about talking to a salesperson. As a result, sales professionals can't just assume that the selling conversation can start with a product demo or an introduction to the levels of service they offer—they need to understand where buyers are in their journey and meet them where they are. Today's savvy customers aren't looking for someone who will simply belch out a lot of specs and data about their product and then ask for a signature on the dotted line. They're looking for someone who can add value to the sales conversation by sharing insight and advice. They're looking for someone who can help them make an intelligent purchasing decision. They're looking for someone who has taken the time to discover their needs. They're looking for someone who has evolved beyond order taker to trusted adviser.

So, in Chapter 1, we'll look at how to sell to today's customers. Doing so in a competitive, evolving marketplace requires creating an effective selling relationship that incorporates Critical Selling skills and best practices, all with an eye toward developing the kind of trust and credibility that allows sales professionals in any industry, whether B2B or B2C, to think, act, and communicate in a customer-focused way throughout the selling cycle. That's because, regardless of all the changes in the world of sales, the customer is still at the center of any successful sales approach. Top performers understand that they need to change if they want to keep up with the ways in which customers, too, are changing.

Of course, change doesn't just happen overnight. So, the first step in all of this is to embrace the change that is required. This means that sales professionals need to have the right mindset when looking to improve performance. They need to be all in when it comes to understanding, accepting, and practicing the Critical Selling framework. Being open-minded to change is critical when it comes to adopting the skills that allow you to continually improve your performance. We'll talk about this in Chapter 2.

In order to sell to today's buyers, top-performing sales professionals know that they have to deliver a differentiated experience and find unique ways to add tangible value throughout the buying process. But first, if you truly want to become a top performer, you have to believe in the process and make a commitment to it. You have to have the right mindset if you want to accelerate the sales process and close more deals.

That means you have to commit yourself to training and practicing. You need to be open to the possibility that there is always room for improvement in your approach to customers. That's not to say that the experience, insight, or wisdom you've gained during the course of your career is without value. Rather, it means that in today's highly competitive marketplace, it's important to recognize that customers are evolving and that, as a result, sales is evolving. And so you, too, have to evolve if you want to keep up with your customers (and with your competitors). To do that, you need to believe that the process will yield tangible benefits—for you and for your customers.

In Chapter 2, we'll look at the importance of committing to and carefully following the Critical Selling framework. We'll discuss why top performers know that the key to securing more and better deals isn't about "always be closing" but rather about "always be improving." Why? Because best-in-class organizations—and top-performing sales professionals—know that practice is a key component to success.

Change can be difficult. Trial and error as you learn the process might feel clunky. But top performers know that believing in the promise of change, and in following the Critical Selling framework from start to finish, is crucial to making it work. Because the Critical Selling framework isn't a buffet. It's a proven, logical, and practical approach to accelerating the sales process and closing more deals while building credibility with customers and developing lasting, profitable relationships.

Incorporating strategies, skills, and best practices requires planning, which underlies the entire Critical Selling framework. Why? Because planning isn't one step you do at the beginning of the sales process and then check off your to-do list. Top performers know that effective planning matters at every stage during the selling cycle. They also understand that it is important not only to plan ahead for every call but also to reflect afterward. And they understand the benefits of planning and reflecting for each and every call.

Part of planning requires outlining the critical objectives for each call, and in Chapter 3, we'll look at the importance of setting objectives, how doing so helps salespeople better connect with customers, and how it helps accelerate the sales process. We'll also look at a variety of helpful tools and resources that can make planning work for you—and for your customer.

From planning, we move to opening. Solid openings don't happen by chance. They don't begin with a canned line or a memorized script. Through our research, we have found that too many sales reps lean all too often on timeworn pitches when opening the sales conversation with their customers. On the other hand, we've also found that top performers understand the importance of crafting openings that are personalized for each individual customer.

Top-performing sales professionals understand that a solid opening requires specific, intentional steps, things to do in the first few minutes of the call that will set the stage—and the tone—for connecting with the buyer and building the kind of rapport that will put you on the right track to building stronger, longer-lasting relationships with customers.

Top performers understand the benefits of a good opening. They know that it's not about foisting their personalities upon the customer but rather about understanding the customer's style and adapting the conversation accordingly. Sales professionals who perfect the art of opening find that the rest of the selling cycle naturally falls in place.

In Chapter 4, we'll look at the elements of a solid opening. We'll look at how so many salespeople struggle with determining the right thing to say to the customer and with getting the conversation started on the right track, and we'll look at how top performers overcome those struggles in order to successfully open interactions with customers and quickly begin the rapport-building process. We'll also examine how delivering a Legitimate Purpose Statement helps you connect with customers, manage expectations, and successfully direct the sales conversation. We'll discuss the importance of confirming to ensure that you and the customer are on the same page. And finally, we'll look at best practices as well as common missteps in this stage of the sales process.

With a solid opening secured, the next stage in the Critical Selling framework is all about understanding. Our research has revealed that, unfortunately, too many sales reps gloss over this critical step in the selling cycle, sometimes out of haste, sometimes out of laziness, sometimes out of fear. But the discovering phase of the process is critical to understanding your customer and building trust—and getting it right actually helps speed up the entire sales process.

Discovering what the customer needs and what drives his purchasing decision requires salespeople to do two things: ask questions and listen to the answers. Seems simple, but many sales professionals struggle with these two critical skills, for a variety of reasons. Getting this right is crucial, and doing so puts you in a position to connect with the customer, become a trusted adviser, and offer solutions that are tailored to the needs of the customer.

In Chapter 5, we'll look at what it takes to ask the right questions and to become a good active listener. We'll examine critical areas of focus that top performers key in on in order to build a solid understanding of customer needs. And we'll explain how getting the discovering phase right can be a key way to differentiate yourself from the competition. Finally, we'll look at what top performers do in order to get this step right—and where average performers get it wrong.

As we've seen (and will discuss further in the pages to come), today's customers aren't interested in being pitched. Although a lot of sales professionals want to move straight from opening to closing (that old "always be closing" mantra can be difficult to silence), that's almost always a grave mistake. And although a lot of salespeople spend much of their time on perfecting their pitch, presenting a memorized, generic solution almost never works the way you might like to believe it will. The key to presenting successfully is to share a solution that is uniquely tailored to each individual customer.

Top performers know that getting the opening right and getting the discovering phase right pave the way to making presentations that are well-aligned to customers and their needs. So, in Chapter 6, we'll look at how top performers tackle this stage, from planning their approach to tailoring the solution to asking for feedback. Top performers also understand the power of linking, so we'll discuss why linking your solutions to your customer's needs helps provide the confidence each buyer needs to make the purchasing decision—and to be comfortable with that decision. Part of that requires you to understand customer needs, and we'll look at how the critical areas of focus discussed in Chapter 5 come to bear on this phase of the process. We'll also look at some best practices (such as presenting persuasively) and common pitfalls (such as presenting by rote).

It should be clear by now that the Critical Selling framework does not espouse the old saying that you should "always be closing," an obsolete phrase that for far too long has served as the mantra for sales professionals. Closing should be neither pushy nor passive. Nor should it come as a surprise. In fact, top performers who practice the skills in Critical Selling understand that by planning each sales call, delivering a solid opening, discovering the customer's needs, and presenting persuasively, closing the deal comes naturally because they have simply built on the momentum that has already marked the selling cycle.

In Chapter 7, we'll discuss how and when top performers take the opportunity to secure what already has been done. We'll look at the four critical steps to closing well. And we'll look at the benefits of acting as a trusted adviser at this stage, about speaking directly and frankly with your customer, and about being straightforward.

When it comes down to it, closing should come naturally. It shouldn't feel rushed or pressured. Instead, it should capitalize on the momentum you and your customer have created during the entire sales process. In fact, getting everything right up to this point actually makes closing that much better—and that much easier.

Of course, getting everything right doesn't mean you'll never hear another customer tell you "no." Few people like to hear "no"—especially when it comes from a customer. But dealing with objections is part of the game. Top performers understand that objections can come at any point during the selling cycle, and those who follow the Critical Selling framework know that the very process itself can reduce the number of objections. Why? Because asking the right questions, listening to the answers, and tailoring solutions to customer needs goes a long way in addressing the issues that most concern customers, often before they have even voiced those concerns.

Everyone wants to minimize objections, and the Critical Selling framework will help you do just that. In Chapter 8, we'll look at four key skills salespeople can (and should) use to address objections. We'll look at how to handle even those objections that customers have a difficult time articulating. And we'll take a close look at handling price objections, which is one of the trickiest landmines in the selling landscape and one that weighs heavily on the minds of most sales professionals. In addition, we'll discuss why top performers view objections as opportunities rather than obstacles (and why you should, too).

Accepting that it might be time for a new sales approach can be difficult. Change is hard. But top performers who follow the Critical Selling framework understand that it isn't a one-and-done experience. Top performers continually practice planning, opening, discovering, and closing. They reflect and assess. They learn from what works and what doesn't. And, importantly, they keep an open mind to change, to new processes and tools, and to the various evolutions in the world of buying and selling.

Look: we understand that there are a lot of ways to improve sales performance. There are a lot of tools and resources and gadgets and programs that purport to help sales reps win more sales. We know—because research has proven—that the process we'll share with you in these pages is one of the most effective ways to improve sales performance so that you can close more deals, closing them faster and with fewer objections. That's because sales isn't about tools or gadgets or programs. As we said before, sales comes down to the sales professional and the customer—and the interactions between them. Sales is all about executing on the critical moments in the sales process in order to achieve desired outcomes.

Critical Selling provides a proven process that shows sales professionals how to handle those critical moments. This process helps sales professionals improve their customer approach, build trust, shorten the sales cycle, and close more deals. Having trained thousands of sales professionals in the Critical Selling program, and having gained research-driven insight from hundreds of companies and thousands of sales professionals, we've learned a thing or two about what makes the most effective sales approach for today's customers.

Top performers who embrace this process—and practice it regularly—understand that doing so will help their companies, their customers, and their careers. One of the first steps is to understand that having the right mindset is key to improving performance, and we'll look closely at that in the pages that follow. But before we do that, we first need to understand how customers have changed and what that change means for the sales process in general and for sales professionals in particular. We'll look at that next, in Chapter 1.

1

Selling to Today's Buyers: Remain Customer-Focused

MAYBE IT'S CHANGING technology. Maybe it's the still-recovering economy, which in some sectors has yet to bounce back from the Great Recession. Maybe it's increased competition. Whatever the reason, it's useless to deny that sales is changing—and in dramatic ways. Researchers note, for example, that "[c]ompanies are reporting longer sales cycle times, lower conversion rates, less reliable forecasts, and compressed margins."[1]

If the selling landscape is changing, so too is the buying landscape. Buying behavior is changing in numerous ways. Of course, today's buyers have always been and will always be different from the customers of yesterday. From the production era to the sales era to the marketing era to the information era, selling and buying have progressed, evolving with changing times, changing needs, and changing technology. It's no different today—except, perhaps, for the pace of change.

Back in the day, sales professionals held all the cards. If a customer needed something, the sales rep provided all the information, educated the customer, and drove the selling conversation. Oh, how the tables have turned.

Today, customers are in large part driving the selling conversation. In fact, many studies have shown, and thought leaders agree, that customers are much further along in the buying process before engaging the sales professional; some reports indicate that customers are as much as 60 percent of the way through their decision-making process by the time they connect with a sales rep.

The implications of these findings are no less than earthshaking. In addition to changing technology, a challenging economic climate, and increased global competition, sales professionals today now must deal with customers who are much further along in the decision-making process, who are much more educated, who are technologically savvy, and who are busier than ever. Customers often know what they want and have an idea of what it should cost as well as how long it should take to get it. They know what you and your competitors can offer, and they might even understand how the products and services you can provide vary from your competitors' products and services.

As a result, it's becoming harder and harder to differentiate yourself and your organization by what you sell. Products and features, options and benefits, prices and specials—despite all the various nuances that might make what you sell at least a little bit different from what your competitors are selling, the truth is it is much more difficult to differentiate on these points. Therefore, today's sales professionals face an important challenge: how to differentiate themselves from all the other sales professionals out there who are selling similar products and services for similar prices.

This is a critical point: in order to succeed, today's top-performing sales professionals must find ways to differentiate themselves. They do this by providing value in how they sell, not just by what they sell. They differentiate themselves by how they build credibility with their customers, by how they nurture customer relationships, and by how they become trusted advisors. In doing so, they can better sell to today's demanding buyers.

Throughout these pages, we'll discuss how these changes have affected the selling conversation, and we'll look at how applying the steps in the Critical Selling framework will help you accelerate the sales process and close more deals, all while remaining focused on the customer. We'll look at planning, opening, discovering, presenting, and closing. And we'll look at overcoming objections. But for now, let's focus on what it takes to sell to today's customer. Because the bottom line is that, despite all the changes, selling is still all about the customer.

That means that today's sales professionals have to focus on the customer. Our research has shown that top performers do several key things to remain customer-focused: they use the right sales approach in dealing with customers at whatever stage they are in their decision-making process. They understand how customers perceive them. And, finally, they work to become trusted advisors. But before they can do any of that successfully, they first have to recognize (and accept) the fact that buyers have changed.

Recognize That Buyers Have Changed

Yesterday's paradigms and yesterday's customers and yesterday's selling approaches no longer apply. Sales and selling are evolving, largely because buyers and buying are evolving. In many cases, buyers are bringing sales reps in much later in the process (the extent to which this happens depends in large part on the complexity of the sale). By some measures, most of the traditional sales process is already done by the time a customer even contacts a sales rep. *Forbes* recently noted, for instance, that about "57 percent of the sales process [has] just disappeared."[2]

Faced with such data, it is useless to deny the facts that sales is changing and that customers have changed. Today's customers have little desire to have their hands held by sales reps who usher them through a lengthy decision-making process. Rather, buyers already have access to a lot of information, and chances are they've figured out their needs (or at least they think they've figured out their needs) before they've even reached out to you. Many likely have even already begun considering specific products or services that could meet their needs, solely based on what they've learned about your company.

Customers can do this because there's so much information out there. Your website; your competitors' websites; industry websites; online social media; traditional media; online, personal, and professional references; and so much more: all of these sources provide customers with avenues to conduct their own research in order to determine what products and services are available to meet their needs. As such, customers are doing much of the legwork that sales reps used to do. And, as a result, the customer may well be further along in the process than sales professionals are used to.

Not only have customers done much of the research but they're also often crafting their own solutions. The research they've conducted and the information they've gleaned from various sources allow them to identify their needs and determine what products and solutions will meet those needs. Today's customers know what they need, they know what they want, and they know how to get it. Furthermore, today's buyers not only know that there are various options available to them but also may even understand how they vary from one another. They have the ability to do the research and at times can determine what the points of differentiation are on price, features, and benefits.

In addition to all of this, buyers are busier than ever—just like everyone else. We're all doing more with less, working on tight deadlines, solving problems in a 24/7 world from which we can rarely, if ever, disconnect. Like the rest of us, buyers are busy and demanding. They have less time to spend (and less inclination to spend time) with salespeople.

Faced with all of these changes, top-performing sales professionals recognize that their world has changed. Top performers don't waste time pining away for the good old days when they could share select, scripted information with less knowledgeable buyers. They don't bother to "always be closing" or go in for the hard sell. Instead, they accept the fact that buyers have changed and that, as a result, they have to change, too. Sales and selling must evolve along with buyers and buying.

With that, top performers understand that today's buyers want salespeople who are ready, willing, and able to meet them where they are in the sales process. They don't want a sales rep who will waste their time going over ground they've already covered on their own. Instead, today's top-performing sales professionals understand that in order to sell to today's demanding customers, they have to adopt a new approach.

Use the Right Sales Approach

Today's customers have no desire to waste their limited time with salespeople who cannot provide tangible value. They have less need to be educated. And they are not at all inclined to deal with sales reps who are more intent on selling a truckload of widgets than they are on solving the customer's needs. So today's salespeople have to use the right approach when dealing with today's buyers.

As much as things have changed, as much as buying and selling have evolved, the right approach remains a customer-focused approach. Today's sales professionals still need to ask questions, listen to the answers, and confirm understanding in each and every dealing with their customers. They also have to be conscious of where the customer already is in the sales process. They have to understand—and appreciate—how much legwork the customer has already done. But, perhaps most important, they have to remember that the customer is still at the center of the right sales approach.

Top-performing sales professionals make it known to their customers that the buyer's needs come first. They put the customer's needs before their own, and they are determined to help solve the customer's problems. They understand their primary role is to help their customers achieve their desired outcomes.

This focus has to be at the center of any sales approach—and it has to be genuine. Top performers aren't putting on an act when they tell their customers that they want to help them find the right solution. They sincerely want to help. Good thing, too, because today's savvy customers can tell when sales reps are insincere. They can sniff out when a sales rep is more focused on making a sale than on providing a solution and helping the customer.

So, instead of launching full-bore into a scripted sales approach, top performers use a customer-focused approach. They seek to have a full understanding of the customer's needs because they know that it is those very needs that drive buying—and selling—opportunities. In order to address the customer's needs, you need to get to know your customer, digging deep so you can discover what it is that's driving the purchase decision; what the customer values most; and what his needs, priorities, and goals are. Despite all the changes in buying behavior, that hasn't changed.

In fact, it's more important than ever. Asking questions in order to discover more about your customer's known and unknown needs, actively listening to the answers, and understanding where the customer is in the buying process are critical components of successful selling to today's buyer. Only in uncovering this crucial customer information will you be able to devise the right solutions that meet his needs. Only then can you bring your expertise, insights, and ideas to the table, helping your customer in ways your competitors simply cannot.

Buyers might well have access to more information than ever before. They might well do more research and, as a result, have a better sense of the solutions that can help them meet their needs. But that doesn't mean they're always right or that they're not open to other ideas, further insight, or useful advice. That's where you come in.

Our research shows that buyers value those sales professionals who can bring these attributes to the sales process. No longer can you just ask the customer what he wants and fill out the order form. It's critical to show the customer that you can be of value as a knowledgeable, helpful sales professional who will carefully evaluate the customer's needs, offer credible insight, and provide valuable advice.

It's in this that you demonstrate what makes you different from—and better than—the competition. Top-performing sales professionals are well-educated about their own products and services. They know their organizations inside out. They also are well-informed about their competitors and their industry in general. In asking thoughtful questions and actively listening to the answers, they develop a deep understanding of their customers. As such, they become the point of differentiation. You can do the same. As a top performer, you can offer added value in your expertise, uncovering of unknown needs, offering of insight and advice that you—and only you—can provide the customer.

You might like to believe that your company offers a truly special product or service, one that is so unique that no other organization comes close. But the truth is that as quickly as your company offers a new feature, your competition is trying to one-up you. However unique you think your product or service is, your competitors are working on replicating that same product or service—and trying to go you one better. The one thing that you can offer that no one else can is yourself. Customer-focused sales professionals who succeed in today's changing marketplace understand that they can provide unparalleled value in the form of their approach.

Of course, they also understand that knowing their customers at a deep level and offering sage advice can't take forever. Today's customers are busier than ever, and there's nothing that turns off a customer more than a sales professional who wastes their time. Top-performing sales professionals respect their customers' limited time. They take the time to plan for each and every selling conversation. They engage in the right activities before, during, and after every sales interaction in order to maximize the limited time they have with their customers.

We'll talk more in the chapters to come about how following the Critical Selling framework will help you save time (for yourself and for your customers), but it's important to note for now that sales professionals should use their time wisely by, for example, researching their customers so that they don't waste precious moments asking for information that easily could have been found out ahead of time. They also should take the time to prepare presentations that are carefully tailored to each customer's needs, avoiding superfluous information that has little or no bearing on the precise solution that will meet the customer's objectives.

Respecting the customer's time, offering keen insight, providing helpful advice, understanding that the customer might have already done a substantial amount of legwork—all of that plays into using a customer-focused approach to sell to today's buyer. It also helps customers perceive you as someone they can rely on and someone they can trust. And in a day and age when customers might not need you as much as or in the same way that they once did, that perception is crucial.

Know How Your Customers Perceive You

How a customer perceives you and the relationship you have together has a significant impact on whether you win a deal and book the sale. Few customers want to deal with an automaton who fills out purchase orders, completes invoices, and arranges to ship orders. Today's customers are looking for someone they can rely on to provide them with crucial information, keen insight, and expert advice that will help them make important purchasing decisions.

Most of us would like to believe that we offer superior service to our customers. But what really matters is what our customers think of us and how they would describe the relationship they have with us. Through our research, we have identified four different and distinct relationship levels that sales professionals can earn with their customers. At each level, the actions, behaviors, and values displayed by sales professionals vary—as do the ways in which customers perceive, value, and trust sales professionals. As shown in

Figure 1.1   The Relationship Continuum

Figure 1.1, the Relationship Continuum identifies those four levels as order taker, friendly salesperson, effective salesperson, and trusted advisor.

It's critical that you understand these levels, and so we define them in detail here:

Order Taker

- Has zero understanding of customer needs
- Does not focus on connecting with or developing relationships with customers
- Is focused on closing the sale without consideration of customer needs
- Does not challenge the customer's thinking or offer options and alternatives
- Does not offer any insights or ideas on the application of products or services

Friendly Salesperson

- Has limited understanding of customer needs
- Is slightly focused on connecting with or developing relationships with customers
- Stays focused on closing the sale with limited consideration of customer needs
- Has slight willingness to challenge the customer's thinking and rarely offers options and alternatives
- Offers very few insights or ideas on the application of products or services

Effective Salesperson

- Has a strong understanding of known customer needs (needs the customer is aware of)
- Remains focused on connecting with and developing relationships with customers
- Strongly considers customer needs when making recommendations in the sales process
- Is willing to challenge the customer's thinking and offer options and alternatives when customers seem open to other ideas
- Offers some insights or ideas on the application of products or services

Trusted Advisor

- Has complete understanding of customer needs (known and unknown needs)
- Deems connecting with and developing relationships with customers of the utmost importance
- Makes customers' needs the number-one priority in the sales process (willing to walk away from a sale)
- Is always willing to challenge the customer's thinking and offer options and alternatives, no matter how strong the customer's opinions
- Always seeks to offer insights or ideas on the application of products or services

Sales professionals who aim to sell to today's demanding, busy customers must strive to become trusted advisors if they want to succeed. In fact, in order to become a top performer, it's critical to work on the skills and best practices that will position you as a trusted advisor. You can't be one without the other: top performers are trusted advisors, and trusted advisors are top performers. It's critical to achieve the highest level of credibility and trust with your customers so that you can accelerate the sales process and close more deals—and become a top-performing sales professional.

Critical Moment: Put Your Customers First

Sales professionals who wish to succeed with today's buyers know they have to focus on customer needs. They put the customer first. Customer-focused selling acknowledges that the customer is at the core of each and every sales interaction. Focusing on the customer and how you can meet her needs (rather than simply on closing deals) helps you earn trust, accelerate the sales process, and close more deals.

Customer-focused selling is an intentional approach and a crucial component of the Critical Selling framework. We've identified a few tactics that can help you put your customer and her needs first:

- **Address Your Customer's Priorities.** Remember that no sales interaction is about you or your goals or your quotas or your schedule. It's about the customer, her priorities, her goals, her values, and her time. Don't assume that you know what she needs or when she needs it. Discuss her priorities with her. And the only way to find out what your customer needs is to ask questions and listen to the answers.
- **Make Sure You Understand What Your Customer Is Telling You.** Customer-focused selling requires sales professionals to continually confirm understanding with their customers. We'll talk a lot about the importance of confirming in the chapters to follow, and that's because it goes a long way in building trust between you and your customer. For now, note that when it comes to meeting your customer's needs, you can do that only when both of you are on the same page as to what those needs are.
- **Share Your Expertise and Your Insight.** If all a customer wanted to do was place an order, she could order her truckload of widgets online, saving herself and you a lot

(continued)

(*continued*)

of time and energy. Remember that your customers are looking to you to add value to the sales process. That means you have to dig deep and listen carefully to what your customers are telling you so that you can analyze the customer's situation, assess her needs, and provide valuable insight and helpful advice. Doing so goes well beyond mentioning features and benefits your customer might not be aware of to offering the expertise and opinions that only you can share.

■ **Use Your Customer's Time Wisely.** When it comes to earning trust and building credibility with your customers, nothing can derail that faster than wasting your customers' time. Don't waste time telling your customer what she likely already knows. Remember that she's likely done research into you, your organization, and your product and service. Don't regurgitate features and benefits that she's already aware of. Instead, focus on discussing what she doesn't know, which might well include things she doesn't even know she doesn't know (those "unknown unknowns"). Ask thoughtful questions, listen attentively to the answers, and confirm details with your customer during every selling conversation.

No one can build trust and earn credibility with their customers unless they put their customers first. It's simply not possible otherwise. If you want to become a top-performing trusted advisor, it's critical that you address your customer's needs and make sure you understand those needs, all while respecting her time. Do that and you'll be on your way to building the kind of trust that moves you in the right direction along The Relationship Continuum.

Become a Trusted Advisor

Trusted advisors go well beyond simply providing specs and product data to offering valuable information. Trusted advisors identify needs and seek to tailor solutions that fit those needs—both known and unknown (i.e., those needs that customers need help in identifying and articulating). Trusted advisors are more than salespeople. They're something different. Trusted advisors are those professionals whom customers trust and rely on for opinions, insight, ideas, and advice. They help educate their customers so that they can make the best possible purchasing decisions.

This is all great for the customer, and it's great for you, too. There are a number of benefits associated with being a trusted advisor. When your customer perceives you as a trusted advisor, you:

- Get more access to important customer information, which will better help you tailor a unique solution to fit his needs;
- Get more time to spend with the customer, who values your insight and advice and wants to take the time to discuss your ideas;
- Get access to more people who are involved in the decision-making process;
- Get the first call when the customer is looking to buy again, which goes far in helping to accelerate the sales process and close more deals.

Of course, we know we're not coining a phrase here; the notion of "trusted advisor" has been around for a while. For example, nearly two decades ago, in their 2000 book *The Trusted Advisor*, authors David Maister and Charles Green explained that, without trust, no salesperson can achieve his goals—but that when trust is established between customer and salesperson, just about anything is possible.[3]

We couldn't agree more, and our own research shows that trust remains of the utmost importance to the sales process. In fact, at a time when customers are smarter, savvier, and busier than ever, trusted advisors are more important than ever before. Regardless of all the changes facing the industry, the importance of achieving the status of trusted advisor has not changed. What has changed is how you go about earning that status.

Following the Critical Selling framework discussed in these pages will help you earn the status of trusted advisor. Adopting the skills discussed in these pages will help you create the kind of effective selling relationships that benefit your customers and your organization. And accepting that today's buyers have changed will make that process a lot easier for you.

Of course, it won't happen overnight. But if you commit to the process, follow the Critical Selling framework, and remain customer-focused, you'll find that, over time, you'll very likely earn the distinction of trusted advisor. And, once you have obtained that distinction, you'll see higher levels of performance. You'll close more deals, and you'll do so more quickly and with fewer objections.

Top performers understand that none of this happens just because they wish it to. It takes an open mind. It takes an "always be improving" mentality. We'll talk about the importance of having an open mind and adopting an always-be-improving attitude next, in Chapter 2.

Critical Selling: Lessons Learned

- Changing times have led buyers to change their behavior, which means that sales professionals also need to change if they wish to keep up with their customers—and their competitors.
- Top performers also know that the right sales approach remains one that is customer-focused. The customer remains at the center of each and every sale.
- Top-performing sales professionals understand that products and services vary little from one company to the next. Because of that, they make themselves the point of differentiation, sharing

their unique expertise, insight, and advice with customers in order to craft tailored solutions that meet their needs.

- How your customer perceives you can make or break a deal. Sales professionals who earn the title of trusted advisor are best able to meet their customers' needs, all while accelerating the sales process and closing more deals.

2

The First Step Is to Believe: Change Your Mindset

WE KNOW THAT sales is evolving and that buyers are changing. In fact, sales is always evolving. New products and services are constantly being brought to the marketplace. Every organization is trying to outflank its competition, whether through new products and services or through new sales and marketing efforts or through new customer-focused initiatives. Similarly, customers themselves are changing—and faster than ever. How they shop, where they shop, and the tools they shop with are evolving along with new technology. Why they buy, how they decide to buy, and their buying expectations are changing as well.

It's challenging enough to keep up with customers and competitors—much less to stay a step ahead of them. But if you want to have even a hope of keeping up with the changes that every sales professional faces today, and if you want to be a top performer, it's critical that you be open-minded, welcome continual improvement, and remain willing to adjust your sales approach to meet the needs of the market and of your customers.

Over the years, in consulting with countless sales professionals across dozens of industries and selling environments, we've seen a lot of what works and what doesn't when it comes to improving performance and sales effectiveness. We've identified scores of best practices as a result of our ongoing research. That research clearly shows that continuous improvement is critical when it comes to accelerating sales. So is an open mindset. In fact, you can't have continuous improvement without first adopting an open mindset that welcomes opportunities to grow.

Improving sales doesn't happen overnight, and it doesn't happen by simply following a cookie-cutter, step-by-step recipe for change. Processes are important, of course, and the Critical Selling framework that we'll be sharing with you in these pages will, when followed correctly, help you accelerate the sales process and close more deals. But you can't do anything until you are truly open to change.

The key to change—and to getting improved results—is to effect positive shifts in behavior. This doesn't necessarily have to happen all at once. One change at a time can yield dramatic results. In fact, a little change at a time can be not only easier but more encouraging when it comes to goals. Consider, for instance, the difference between telling yourself you need to lose fifty pounds (a daunting task for anyone) and aiming to shed a pound a week for a year. The latter option—a little bit of change over a period of time—is much more feasible.

Just as successful dieters accept that a lot of little changes can make big, lasting, and positive differences in their health regimens, we see in top performers a willingness to incorporate change into their professional regimens. They consistently embrace new learning, practice new approaches, and look for new ways to grow professionally. Top performers understand that in a world that is constantly changing, they need to change, too. They need to adapt to new buying behaviors. They need to accept that competition is coming from all corners of the globe.

Top performers also understand that it's never safe to rest on their laurels. There's no such thing as standing still—you're either forging ahead or falling behind. Knowing this, top performers understand the need to keep up with their training, regardless of how much tenure they might have or how successful they've been in the past. Top performers are willing to grow. They're willing to develop themselves. They adopt a positive mindset that allows them to see opportunities in obstacles. Believing that you can change for the better is a critical first step when it comes to becoming a top-performing sales professional.

Mind Your Mindset

Having the right mindset goes beyond having a cheerful, positive outlook (although that's important, too) to being open-minded about constantly learning and adapting to the always-changing sales landscape. Top performers are open-minded when it comes to continual improvement. They believe in consistently working on their craft, they're open to new ideas, and they have a positive outlook on continually learning and implementing new approaches in the pursuit of improved sales performance. Top performers actively search for new ways to do things better.

In observing thousands of sales professionals across hundreds of organizations, we have identified scores of characteristics that are consistent among them. For example, top performers are consistently looking for ways to improve and get better. They're always looking to grow. When they think back to when they started out in their careers, they recognize that over the years they've grown professionally by asking for advice, reading widely, keeping up on industry trends, and seeking training. Today's top-performing sales professionals, regardless of tenure, are always looking to improve. Why? Because they know that success in the past doesn't guarantee success in the future. They also realize that it can be way too easy to become relaxed, to get too comfortable, or to become regimented in their approach to sales. When that happens, it's easy to become close-minded to new ideas. When that happens, it's easy to stop learning new things, to quit working on their craft, to stop practicing.

Resistance and complacency are not at all uncommon among lower performers. Our research has revealed that lower performers—those sales reps who typically find themselves ranked among their colleagues as having the fewest sales, the smallest sales, and infrequent sales—really don't want to change. They view change as a lot of work, work that might well be undertaken with little payoff. They resist change, whether out of fear or laziness or arrogance. This can manifest itself in an attitude that makes it clear to everyone around them that they are not willing to make a change.

While top performers welcome change and are open-minded to the potential benefits of employing a new approach to accelerating the sales process and closing more deals, lower performers often actually work to sabotage efforts to change. While top performers are finding ways to make change work for them and their customers, lower performers often spend much of their time trying to justify why they shouldn't change. We've also seen that lower performers give up on change before even giving it a chance to work.

You can see here how mindset matters. Top performers are open-minded to change, and they generally view it in a positive way. They are optimistic about the improved results that change might drive. Lower performers, on the other hand, are closed-minded when it comes to change. They prefer the status quo and are uncomfortable with change, which they often see as unnecessary. Lower performers find it difficult, if not impossible, to see how change will benefit them.

We understand that change can be difficult, but we also know that it's critical to embrace change if you want to be a top performer. Going about that need not be intimidating. In fact, McKinsey & Company, a global management consulting firm, notes (and we agree) that in order to accept change and enthusiastically adapt the new approaches that will allow you to improve performance, just two things must happen: you have to understand how your actions will affect outcomes, and you have to believe that all this change is worthwhile.[1] Top performers understand this implicitly, and what's more is that they are open-minded to change because they appreciate the potential benefits of implementing change. They look at change through a lens of optimism, believing that the anticipated outcomes of change will be of benefit to them, their customers, and their organizations.

Top performers also understand that change simply for the sake of change rarely sticks. In order to enjoy lasting improvement, it's critical to believe in it. Top performers trust that making the kind of adjustments that will allow for that change is worthwhile. In short, they feel the need for change, and they feel motivated to change.

The kind of motivation needed to embrace change often stems from an understanding of the benefits of change. For sales reps who are looking to become top-performing sales professionals, there are many benefits of following a proven process designed to accelerate the sales process and close more deals. Let's look at just some of the benefits of following the Critical Selling framework:

- Stronger, longer-lasting relationships with new and existing customers
- Accelerated sales cycles with higher win rates
- Improved confidence when dealing with customers
- Higher levels of trust and credibility with your customers
- Reduced objections and negative pushback from customers

Positive outcomes such as these motivate top-performing sales professionals in organizations we've worked with (Alliant Credit Union and TIAA-CREF, for example) because they can see how embracing the kind of change that results in these benefits is worthwhile.

Here's the thing: the things you've done along the way won't keep you successful forever. It's critical to continue to hone your craft, learn new skills, and pay attention to how the industries you sell to—and the sales profession itself—are evolving. Because the truth is that things are always changing: Buyers are changing. Products are changing. The sales profession is changing. You need to adapt to these changes—and to all the changes that will keep coming down the line. The people who stay great at sales are the ones who want to improve, are open to change, work on their skills, and practice, practice, practice.

Always Be Improving

Top performers know that the key to securing more and better deals isn't about "always be closing"; rather, it's about "always be improving." Best-in-class organizations, for example, emphasize practicing core skills because they want to instill institutional competency across their employees. Why? Because best-in-class organizations know that practice is a key component to success. The same is true for best-in-class sales professionals.

Top performers are always looking for ways to improve their performance. They understand that the key to always be improving is to investigate new ideas, assess new approaches, implement those changes that seem most appropriate, and put in the work to see it through. That doesn't mean they jump on every new sales technique that pops up. But it does mean that they keep practicing on honing and improving their skills. They're open-minded not only to the notion of change but also to the fact that change takes time, effort, and practice (as well as patience).

Oddly enough, although we hear throughout our lives that practice makes perfect, society tends to value what it perceives as effortless success. Sales is no exception when it comes to valuing this perception. Sometimes we call this "talent" or "luck." We admire that salesperson who has a gift for gab, who is a people person, who can sell ice to an Eskimo, as the saying goes. But there's much more to it than that. Top-performing salespeople don't rely on talent alone, and they don't believe that success comes without effort.

Indeed, the notion of easy success can actually be more negative than positive. Duke University researchers, for example, have found that the idea of "effortless perfection" can be stifling and suffocating and that it can hinder development.[2] This perception can make it difficult to embrace the notion of "always be improving," even though practice is critical when it comes to the world of sales performance.

Practice is fundamental in continuous improvement, although we realize that it might be easier said than done for some people. Practice takes time—time a lot of busy salespeople might believe they don't have, or time they don't think they need to invest. But time is the very thing they should, indeed, set aside if they want to become top performers in their organizations. You can practice with your peers, your manager, in training, and even by yourself. Or you could practice on your customers, with greater risks at play. The choice is yours.

Let's turn for a moment to the world of sports, which is analogous to business in many ways, not the least of which relates to the importance of practice. The best athletes aren't necessarily the ones with natural talent. Not that talent doesn't matter, but evidence has shown that the greats are those who are dedicated to practicing because they want to improve their game. Wayne Gretzky. Ted Williams. Venus and Serena Williams. Kobe Bryant. The list goes on and on. But perhaps one of the greatest athletes of all time is Michael Jordan. The Chicago Bulls point guard didn't start out his career as a basketball player at the top. In fact, he was cut from his high school varsity basketball team. So what did Jordan do? He embraced discipline and practice. Jordan was known for going back to the court after losing games and practicing shots for hours on end.[3]

Practice, however, isn't just about putting in the time. Jordan understood that practice for the sake of practice didn't matter if he wasn't improving. His goal wasn't to spend time shooting free throws on the practice court. It was to sink every free throw on the practice court so he could implement that skill with success on game day. He understood that the key to continual improvement was to practice the right skills in the right way. As Jordan has said, "You can practice shooting eight hours a day, but if your technique is wrong, then all you become is very good at shooting the wrong way."

You don't want to become very good at approaching customers in the wrong way. Whether in basketball or baseball or manufacturing or sales or whatever, practicing the "right" things in the right ways is critical when it comes to success. Top-performing athletes don't just get good and go out and win games—and neither do top-performing salespeople just get good and go out and win sales: practice is key.

When it comes to sales, what does it mean to practice? It's not like you can go out to the selling court and volley a few sales pitches back and forth with one of your competitors. Rather, practice for sales professionals means conducting industry research, studying the competition, improving product knowledge, leveraging sales tools, working on your presentation skills, learning how to be a better listener, and so on. The truth is that there's no shortage of areas where you can seek to hone your skills in order to keep improving—because you should always be improving. There is a misconception in sales that once you've had success, you're good enough, and so you can just keep on doing what you have been doing. But the truth is that those who are the best are the ones who continue to work on improving their skills. They are committed to practicing because good sales is about sustained effort. You don't just learn how to sell and then stop learning or trying to improve.

Critical Moment: Avoid the Tenure Trap

It's a common misconception that tenure = experience = performance. Many people think that if someone has a lot of experience, well, then, she must be a top performer.

But that just isn't true.

Just because Jane has posted great numbers in the past, it doesn't necessarily guarantee that she'll keep posting great numbers in the future.

It's easy to have preconceived notions about the skills, abilities, and aptitude of tenured professionals (e.g., those who have a good decade's worth of experience). Many people—including tenured professionals themselves—believe that these professionals are full of talent, are skilled at their work, and have a natural ability to get the job done.

Such notions can make it difficult to embrace the mindset that allows for the kind of change that helps improve performance.

This is really just a form of resistance, and we see resistance to change in a lot of sales professionals, especially those who've been around the block a few times. But it's a trap to believe that tenured professionals can't keep learning, can't keep embracing new approaches, can't keep improving. That trap is a closed mindset, and that closed mindset more often than not leads to diminishing performance. In order to avoid falling into the tenure trap, it's critical to avoid some common pitfalls:

- **Don't Believe That Tenure = Fully (and Forever) Trained.** Even the most experienced sales rep needs ongoing sales training and coaching. No matter how good the performance (real or perceived) of a tenured salesperson, there is always room for improvement. The sales professional who has an open mindset is the one who will benefit from embracing the kind of change that will lead to improved performance. Keep in mind the importance—and utility—of ongoing training and lifelong learning so that you can always be improving.

- **Don't Let Complacency Get the Best of You.** It's critical to embrace a positive mindset that is open to the idea of continuous improvement, and this is especially true for tenured salespeople. We see new sales reps who start out their careers constantly looking for ways to improve. They try out new approaches. They keep up with their training. They study industry trends and fads. They understand that things are constantly changing—products, approaches, buying behavior, and so on—and they do whatever it takes to keep up. All too often, however, tenured sales pros start not

(continued)

(*continued*)

keeping up. They start cutting corners. They start thinking they know everything. They fall into the status quo trap, staying stagnant while everything around them changes. When this happens, performance falters. Don't be that person. Do whatever it takes to avoid becoming lazy or complacent by seeking out new opportunities to grow.

■ **Don't Sabotage Yourself.** It's natural to resist change. It's hard work. It takes time. It can be scary. It's full of uncertainty. Top performers understand this, and they work hard to overcome these feelings. Don't succumb to feelings of dread, egotism, or laziness, which might lead you to shy away from change or avoid it altogether. Sales professionals who resist change will quickly fall behind, and they end up sabotaging their own careers by eschewing opportunities that could help them improve their performance.

■ **Don't Think That You're Done Learning.** What top performer has ever said, "Great! I've made it. I'm good enough. I can quit learning now," and then called it a day? No one. That's who. Top performers understand that life-long learning and continuous improvement are critical components of the kind of positive mindset that keeps them at the top of their game.

Stay Patient through Change

Change can be difficult. As you learn a new process and implement the changes that go along with it, what once was familiar to you might suddenly feel clunky. Let's say, for example, that you want to work on your golf swing—you have had enough with all the hooks and slices. You realize that it's time to go back to basics and work on your mechanics. In no time, you're aching in muscles you didn't even know you had. Your shots are still going all over the place, and in some cases, they're even worse than they were before. Your friends are starting to call you "Double Bogey."

At this point you have two choices: you can quit and revert to your old swing and accept the level of player that you are, or you can persevere with the new swing in the belief that the change will soon feel like second nature and that it will get your game where you want it to be.

Just as with any kind of change, some people might begin to institute new approaches advocated in the Critical Selling framework only to find that they might not work perfectly on the first try—and then give up. Most of us resist change, at least at first or for a little while. It's easy to make excuses and give yourself permission to go back to the old ways. It's easy to revert to comfortable (i.e., bad) habits when expected results don't materialize instantaneously. That happens to all of us. It happens in sports (my old swing was working just fine), in dieting (I can go ahead and eat that double bacon cheeseburger), and in business (our current procedures are adequate, thank you very much). Researchers Emily Lawson and Colin Price note that "employees will alter their mindsets only if they see the point of the change and agree with it—at least enough to give it a try."[4] You have to keep trying.

Top performers understand that change is necessary if they want to improve their performance. They have the mindset that accepts that change takes time, and they realize that change will take some work, that it doesn't happen overnight. Top performers understand that change can be a little uncomfortable, but they accept that because they know change will lead them to a better place in the end. Because of that, top performers are as persistent as they are patient. They push through the discomfort that often accompanies change. They know that they have to keep practicing if they want to make a change for the better.

Continual improvement requires practice and an open mindset. Having an open mind means that you have the willingness to change. Top performers understand that if they really want to accelerate the sales process and close more deals, they have to commit to practicing all the skills in the Critical Selling framework—all the skills with every customer during every sales interaction.

Mindset matters here, because you have to be all in when it comes to understanding and applying the Critical Selling framework. You don't get to pick and choose from among the various skills and strategies and best practices; they all build on one another. You can't jump from delivering a solid opening to presenting your solution. You can't deliver a solid presentation without first discovering key information about your customer. Rather, you have to embrace the entire thing, from start to finish.

We are proud to continue to work with thousands of top-performing sales professionals at organizations such as American Express, Catalent, MGM Resorts International, and TripAdvisor, and we have gathered data and insight about skills, strategies, and best practices. We've looked at what works and what doesn't when it comes to accelerating the sales process and closing more deals—everything from planning to building relationships to becoming a trusted advisor. Our research has revealed that following the process is crucial when it comes to getting sales right. And that means not just following the process today with one client, but forever with every client.

Top performers understand that fully committing to the process is crucial when it comes to connecting with customers and improving sales. If you want to become a top performer, if you want to accelerate the sales process and close more deals, you have to believe in the process and make a commitment to yourself to embrace the kind of change that will allow you to improve your behavior and, as a result, your sales record. That means you have to change your mindset.

Having an open, positive mindset is critical, because nothing will happen if you don't first commit to yourself. And that means that you have to embrace new learning and new approaches that will allow you to reach higher goals. Indeed, in a report on the importance of changing attitudes and behavior in order to improve performance, researchers at McKinsey note that "employees may need to adjust their practices or to adopt new ones in line with their *existing* mindsets in order to reach, say, a new bottom-line target."[5] We couldn't agree more.

Embracing change, adjusting existing practices, adopting new approaches . . . all of that means that you have to commit yourself to training and practicing. You need to be open to the possibility that there is room for improvement in your approach to customers. That's not to say that the experience, insight, and wisdom you've gained during the course of your career is without value. Rather, it means that in today's highly competitive marketplace, it's important to recognize that customers are evolving and that, as a result, sales also is evolving. You have to keep up with your customers. And to do that, you need to believe that embracing change is first about adopting a new mindset.

Making a change for the better is critical if you want to be a top performer who can keep up not only with the competition but also with today's demanding customers. The Critical Selling framework—which focuses on the skills required in planning, opening, discovering, presenting, and closing—ensures that you practice the right skills in order to accelerate the sales process, reduce the number of objections you face, and ultimately close more deals. But getting each phase of the process right takes dedication. It takes practice. It may take some trial and error to see what works for you and your customers in their particular situations. And, perhaps above all, it takes a mindset that accepts the necessity of change, embraces the need to keep improving, and understands the need to stay patient through change. By following the process—and by keeping an open mind—you'll be in a better position to consistently be a top performer.

Accepting change, adapting the right mindset, and practicing your skills are crucial when it comes to working toward trusted-advisor status and toward becoming a top performer. It also takes planning. Planning is a critical step in the sales process, and we'll discuss that next, in Chapter 3.

Critical Moment: Understand That Resistance Is Futile (and Costly)

"If you do what you've always done, you'll get what you always got."

Although this quote has been variously attributed over the years to Henry Ford, Ed Foreman, Tony Robbins, Mark Twain, and countless others, the message is clear: you can't keep doing what you have been doing and still expect better results.

People are often resistant to change, even though it's happening all around us all the time. You can try to resist with all your might, but change will keep happening whether you're ready or not. Furthermore, the cost of not changing—and not changing fast enough—can be staggering. For instance, research shows that "the pace of change is so fast that technologies and skills to use them become obsolete within five to ten years."[6]

Simply recognizing that it's time for change because you or your organization is stuck in a quagmire can be a big challenge. In fact, studies have shown that "although employers and workers alike realize that they must learn new things, they often don't feel they have the time to do so."[7] Clearly, part of the challenge with committing to learning new things is making the time. Solving those challenges requires admitting that change is needed.

This kind of change doesn't happen just by wishing for it. You have to commit to change. You have to invest in training yourself to adopt a new mindset if you want to close bigger deals. Top performers we've worked with at organizations such as Cartier, Northrop Grumman, and Visa understand that the benefits of accepting change and adopting the Critical Selling framework are well worth it.

But let's turn the tables for a moment. We know that people are resistant to change, for any number of reasons. It takes time, is disruptive, uses up resources, and costs money. But what are the costs of not changing? What is the cost of doing what you've always done?

You have to invest in yourself if you want to become a top-performing salesperson. That means you have to think not just about any out-of-pocket expenses—in dollars or time—that might add up during the course of your education and training but also about the cost of opportunities you might miss out on by not perfecting your skills in advance of your next sales interaction. What are you losing by sticking to your old ways, by not recognizing that customers have changed, by going in for the hard sell, and by trying to close too early or too often?

If, on the other hand, you invest in training and education, if you commit to yourself, and if you follow the entire Critical Selling framework, how much better can you get? By how much might you shorten the sales cycle? How much bigger might your deals become? If, for instance, you should be closing 50 percent of your deals but you're only closing 40 percent, what is the cost of that lost 10 percent?

When it comes to change, resistance not only is futile but also can be costly in terms of protracted selling cycles, lost sales, and lost opportunities.

Critical Selling: Lessons Learned

- Research shows that top-performing sales professionals embrace a positive mindset that leaves them open to change and allows them to grow. They understand that no change will stick without a shift in behavior, and the first step in accepting change is to embrace an open and positive mindset.
- Top-performing sales professionals embrace change, but that doesn't mean they jump in feet first to try every new sales technique that hits the world of sales. Instead, they keep an

open mind, research their options, assess those with the best potential, and stay patient while working through the change.

- Top performers avoid common pitfalls that lower performers often fall into. They understand that being tenured doesn't excuse them from seeking new training opportunities, they don't get complacent or lazy, and they constantly work to keep improving.
- Top-performing sales professionals accept that change is normal— and that it is a necessity if they want to stay on top. Instead of avoiding change, they actively search for new ways of doing things in order to practice their skills and remain at the forefront of their industry.

3

Why Planning Matters:
Determine Your Approach

TOP-PERFORMING SALES PROFESSIONALS know a thing or two about planning. Most important, they know that planning is a skill that must be practiced routinely and consistently in order to increase the effectiveness of their sales calls. All too often, however, the typical sales rep overlooks and undervalues this critical skill, leading him to wing it during sales calls and not get the most out of each interaction.

Planning is frequently discounted by sales professionals, and it becomes easy to lose sight of how much value it provides to the sales interaction. Our own research proves this point: the importance of planning—and the beneficial impacts of it—are frequently overlooked. We see this time and time again. In fact, because of the changes in today's buyer, we see planning as an activity that is more important than ever. Your customers are more informed, and in order to meet them where they are in the buying process and add value to the sales interaction, you need to have a plan.

Studies have shown that there is often a disconnect between planning and sales: people don't plan because they believe (erroneously) that it doesn't matter as much as it actually does.

In fact, according to Harvard Business School professor Frank V. Cespedes, about two-thirds of companies treat planning as a periodic event rather than an ongoing part of the sales process.[1] Planning is not a sometimes thing. It needs to be thought of as a vital part of the process.

Understand That Planning Matters

"A goal without a plan is just a wish."
—Antoine de Saint-Exupéry

Hope is not a strategy, as they say, and no sales professional can just wish his way to closing more deals. In fact, we believe planning to be so important that it is the foundation for the entire Critical Selling framework, as shown in Figure 3.1.

As you can see, planning spans the entire process. It is the foundation of Critical Selling, and our research shows that it is more important now than ever before. Planning matters at every stage in the process, whether before the first call with a prospect, before opening a particular sales interaction, in preparation for making a presentation, or during the final stages of negotiation. Planning is always a critical activity. It's not a step any sales professional should skip at any stage during the sales process.

Figure 3.1   Planning is Critical

Planning before every sales call is critical because today's customers are more informed than ever before—and they expect you to be informed as well, not just about your product or service, but about their organizations and their options and alternatives.

Let's look at this a little more closely. We know that customers are better informed than ever. Chances are they've already done a lot of research before even connecting with you. They've researched you and your company as well as your products or services. They've looked into your competitors and the alternate options that are available to them. Your customers have planned for the sales call with you. They've done their due diligence. In fact, as we discussed in Chapter 1, some research indicates that buyers are as much as 60 percent of the way through the sales process prior to engaging with a sales professional. And even if some customers are not quite that far along, the facts remain that they are doing more and they expect you to be equally prepared. They expect that you will have planned the customer interaction so that you can engage each other in an efficient, effective, meaningful way at whatever point they're at in the sales process.

How much planning and research a sales interaction requires varies depending both on the complexity of the sale and on where you are in the sales process. The more complicated the sale, the more research and planning you'll need to do. A more strategic sale requires more research than a simple sale on a short cycle. A complicated sale might warrant a half hour of research and planning. But if you're selling a product or service that is more transactional in nature to a broad audience, you might spend just a few minutes planning. On the other end of the spectrum, a finalist presentation might require a few hours of planning, and that assumes that you've already done some research along the way. The amount of research you conduct should support what you need to accomplish at any given point in the sales process.

Notice here that we're not saying that you can skip doing any research on a prospect or that you can forget about planning if you're dealing with an existing customer. Planning is an integral part of the entire sales process, with any prospect or customer. You have to plan before each and every interaction with each and every customer, even if you're just spending a few minutes thinking it through.

Think about Planning

The top performers at organizations we've worked with, such as Northrop Grumman and Daimler Trucks North America, are disciplined when it comes to planning. They understand that highly effective planning involves gathering information and determining how best to use it. Planning helps identify the best approach to use with each customer based on where they are in the sales process. As such, it's critical to think these things through.

Planning is, at its heart, a thought process. We encourage sales professionals to set aside some time to really think about each customer and the best sales approach for that particular individual. Planning requires you to carefully consider your customer, his goals, his needs, and his expectations. Regardless of whether the sales interaction is simple or complex, top-performing sales professionals take the time to think about each call.

Our precall planning tool (see Figure 3.2) helps sales professionals spend time planning and thinking about the most important aspects of the sales call. These include:

- People and relationships
- Objectives for each call
- Rapport-building strategies
- Key information to share and find out
- Resources required for the call
- Resistance that might be encountered and strategies to overcome
- Anticipated next steps

Although a written plan might not necessarily be needed for each sales call, planning is always necessary. Writing things down

Critical Selling® Skills Planner

JANEK®
Performance Group

Precall

| Sales Rep Name: | | Call Date: | |
| Account Name: | | Call Time: | |

	Customer Contacts on Call:		Sales Team Contacts on Call:	
#	Name & Title:	Role:	Name & Title:	Role:
1.				
2.				
3.				
4.				
5.				

Critical Selling® Stage: Prospecting ☐ Discovering ☐ Presenting ☐ Closing ☐

What do you want to accomplish on the call? - (SAM)

How will you open the call? (LPS)

How will you build rapport with the customer?

What key things do you know about the customer?

What key things do you want to know about the customer?

What key information do you need to share with the customer?

What resistance might you face? How might you overcome?

What resources will you need for the call?

What are the anticipated next steps?

Figure 3.2 Precall Planner Form.

can be a helpful way to keep track of key issues that characterize each customer and each sales interaction. Thinking about how you will build customer rapport, what key things you want to find out, and what resources you might need for the call will help make sure that you've covered all your bases before you get on the phone or head into a meeting—and that benefits both you and your customer.

Look: no one wants to stumble through a poorly planned sales call. That wastes your time, your organization's time, and most important, your customer's time. Planning makes the difference.

Chances are that you're already thinking about each call (at least let's hope so), even if only in an abstract way. But imagine the chaos that would ensue if you just called up a prospect without any real idea of what you wanted to say, how you wanted to say it, or what you wanted to achieve during the call. That's a surefire way to squander a valuable opportunity.

Planning helps you avoid the kind of aimless sales calls that waste time and even alienate customers. Planning ahead helps you determine what you do know, what you don't know, and what you need to find out. It allows you to act with confidence during the sales interaction, knowing that you have thought it out and prepared well. Planning ensures that you are in the best possible position to meet your objectives.

It's crucial to note here that there's planning and then there's planning smartly. It's important to know what to plan for, which specific areas to investigate, and how to use key research items to get the most out of every sales call. We have identified critical areas of planning and research, areas that will help you make the most impact during each sales interaction. And that starts with knowing what you want to accomplish by the end of the interaction.

Set SAM Objectives

Call objectives are like a compass, helping to guide you toward a desired outcome. Measuring performance against clear objectives not only allows you to determine whether you've been successful in achieving your goals but also helps you plan the right approach to get there. We believe the best objectives have three characteristics: they are specific, appropriate, and measurable (SAM).

Our research shows that top performers who plan their sales interactions using SAM objectives more consistently achieve their call objectives and more confidently move the sales process forward. They understand that SAM objectives not only help them set goals but also help ensure that they've accomplished something of substance during each and every customer interaction. SAM objectives provide the kind of focus that saves time and helps ensure that sales professionals are engaging in productive conversations with customers and are able to ultimately add value to the sales interaction.

Specific. Appropriate. Measurable. Let's dig deeper into these characteristics.

Specific

Specific objectives describe in detail exactly what you want to accomplish. Top performers make the most of outlining specific, immediate objectives. In this context, we're talking about an objective that relates to the very next interaction you will have with a customer. Think about what you would like to accomplish by the end of the interaction and what success looks like at this point in the overall process.

The key is that the objective be specific. Vague objectives such as "improve relationship with Acme Company" don't really help much in terms of setting any kind of actionable direction for the call. "Secure introductions from Bob at Acme with three other people on his team before our next meeting," however, is a much more specific goal. You should be able to look back after each call and know right away whether you've accomplished your objective.

Setting objectives that are clear and specific allows you to assess whether you're making the kind of progress you want to be making.

Top-performing sales professionals evaluate their progress by analyzing what it means if they're truly meeting their goals—or if they aren't. Using the example above—"improve customer relationships"—it is difficult to determine what that means exactly and how to develop a plan to accomplish your objective. On the other hand, if you can detail your objective specifically—"make three more contacts on Bob's team"—you're in a much better position to develop a plan and a clear direction for the call.

Appropriate

In addition to being specific, objectives need to be appropriate. Top-performing sales professionals understand that specificity doesn't make any sense if the objective isn't appropriate for that particular sales interaction. The key is to set specific objectives that are appropriate based on where you and your customer are in the sales process.

That said, we know that determining what is and is not appropriate can often be the most difficult aspect of setting objectives. It can be a challenge to know whether the objectives you're setting are too weak or too strong given where you are in the sales process and on how a given situation is unfolding. You have to think about what can be accomplished under which circumstances and whether your goal is realistic.

The key is to identify the right objective based on where you are in the sales process. So, for instance, it might not be appropriate to try to close the sale on your first call with a new customer. That might well be too strong an objective based on where you are in the process. On the other hand, you might be at a point where it's appropriate to secure an on-site meeting to deliver a presentation to key decision makers and influencers rather than just e-mailing information to your contact so he can share it with his team.

Here's the bottom line: when determining whether an objective is appropriate, consider whether you're asking too much or too little—from your customer, your organization, and yourself—and whether you're making the right ask at the right time.

Measurable

Objectives need to be specific and appropriate, and they also have to be measurable. You have to know whether you've actually accomplished what you set out to do, and you can do that only if your objectives are specific, appropriate, and measurable—otherwise, you're really just guessing, which doesn't do anyone any good.

If, for example, your objective was to, at the end of the sales call, gain agreement from your customer to move forward and sign a contract, you'll know whether you accomplished that—the signed paperwork will be the tangible evidence you need.

Measurable objectives speak to the quantifiable evidence that demonstrates whether you've accomplished what you set out to do. Quantifiable. Evidence. We're not talking about anecdotal evidence. Measurable objectives allow you to monitor your progress as you work through the sales process. The dictum "you can't manage what you can't measure" applies in force here, and top-performing sales professionals understand that measuring progress toward meeting objectives is critical when it comes to accelerating the sales process and closing more deals.

SAM objectives are specific, appropriate, and measurable. They help you focus and plan before each and every customer interaction. This kind of planning helps you identify exactly where you want to go with each customer every time you meet. Setting SAM objectives helps you navigate each sales call and the entire sales process. When you've planned your objectives, you have a better sense of the beginning, middle, and end of each interaction with your customers. When you've articulated to your customers what those objectives are and why they are important, then they, too, know how things will go. In doing so, you better manage their expectations and ensure that you're delivering value to them—all of which accelerates the sales process.

Critical Moment: Articulate Your Objectives

It's critically important that you clearly articulate your objectives to your customer. This is because you need to make sure that you and your customer are in alignment and that your expectations of how each interaction will go are in sync.

How you articulate your objective is equally important as setting the objective itself. We generally don't advise saying outright to a customer, for example, "My objective today is to get this contract signed." Instead, you might say something like, "Today I want to make sure that the solution I outline meets your specific needs and, if so, to agree on the best next step in the process." Remember that how you say something is just as critical as what you say. Your focus should always be on the customer and his needs.

Of course, even the best-laid plans can go awry. If you find that the customer's expectations are out of proportion, you need to be flexible. Respect the customer's expectations while explaining how the objective of the meeting will be of value to him and his organization.

The key here is to communicate with your customer. You might find that your objective is inappropriate in some way. Maybe the timing is off; maybe the topic is off; maybe the scope is off. What's important is that your objective has to work for the customer. It's not about you; it's about the customer.

As a sales professional, you want to meet your own objectives, but doing so should clearly be of value to your customers. Meeting your objectives should be, at its heart, about meeting your customers' needs. How you frame those objectives to your customers is important: it should be all about them.

Plan Ahead and Reflect After

Our research has shown not only that top-performing sales professionals plan each and every interaction with their customers and set SAM objectives but also that they reflect and analyze outcomes.

Reflecting after every sales call is critical. It's important to assess what went well and what didn't. And, because it's so easy to forget critical information the longer you wait to record it, it's important to reflect after every call—right after every call.

We suggest taking a few minutes to write down your reflections after each sales interaction. It's easiest—and most productive—to reflect on a call right away, when it's fresh in your mind. If you try to recall information from a sales call two hours or two days or two weeks later, it's virtually impossible. Top performers understand this and consistently use reflection as a tool to establish better objectives for their next customer interaction.

Our postcall tool (see Figure 3.3) can help you reflect after you interact with your customers. Areas to analyze include:

- Were the SAM objectives for the call reached?
- What went well?
- What could have gone better?
- What challenges did you face?
- What key information did you learn?
- What are the next steps?

Planning and reflecting go hand in hand. As they say, if you don't know where you've been, you can't know where you're going. Without planning, a sales call could easily derail. Without reflecting, it's difficult to know how to plan for the next call. Salespeople who don't take the time to reflect on what they learned right after interacting with a customer risk misremembering what they heard during the conversation and failing to recall critical customer issues.

Critical Selling® Skills Planner

JANEK®
Performance Group

Postcall

Was the objective for the call reached? (SAM)   Yes ☐   No ☐

What went well?

What challenges did you face?

What key information did you learn?

What are the next steps?

What actions need to take place?

Figure 3.3   Postcall Planning Tool.

In addition, if you don't reflect on each customer interaction, it's difficult to evaluate how well you are moving the sales process along or whether you're making the kind of progress you need to. Stalled deals are one of the most difficult things to handle as a salesperson. It is much easier to stay on top of each interaction and capitalize on the momentum you are creating in order to keep the process moving forward. If you don't pay attention to the little things, you could be faced with a stalled deal before you know it. You have to be able to recognize what activities need to take place in order to move the sales process forward. Every time you fail to advance, you decrease the likelihood of securing the sale.

Postcall reflection helps you plan and determine your objectives for the next call so you can accelerate the sales process and close more deals. If you don't do this, you won't be able to adjust and make the next call more productive. Failing to reflect just makes it that much more difficult to plan for the next interaction with your customer.

Reflecting is simply good practice. It's a good routine to establish. It not only makes your sales interactions more efficient and more productive but also provides you with insight into where you might need to adjust your approach. Reflecting then becomes a form of self-coaching, helping you become more aware of the things you do well and the things you do not-so-well.

Planning and reflecting are crucial components of the Critical Selling framework. Top-performing sales professionals who plan each interaction with each customer are better positioned to build credibility, understand customer needs, and accelerate the sales process. Those who take the time to reflect on each sales call can more efficiently and effectively plan for the next call. Top performers understand that planning isn't something you do just once at the early stages of the sales process and then move on; planning must happen at every stage of the process with every customer. Top performers also know that it is critical to plan for each sales call and each selling conversation. Whether planning for an initial call with a new prospect, for a winning presentation, or for closing the deal, it's critical to set SAM objectives and assess progress. Once you have taken the time to plan for the customer interaction, the next step is to deliver a solid opening that gets the sales conversation going in a positive direction, which is where we're headed next, in Chapter 4.

Critical Selling: Lessons Learned

- Today's customers expect that you will have planned the customer interaction so that you can engage each other in a meaningful way. Top-performing sales professionals understand how critical it is to plan for each and every customer interaction, no matter where you are in the sales process—first call or last.

- Planning ahead helps determine what you know about your customers, their needs, and their expectations, as well as what you don't know and what you need to find out. Using the precall planner form can help you focus each customer interaction so that you are more confident, more efficient, and more effective.

- Top-performing sales professionals set clear call objectives, knowing that they help provide focus for every customer interaction, navigate each sales call, and manage overall expectations. SAM objectives provide a specific and repeatable framework for establishing the right objectives in the sales process.

- Planning and reflecting go hand in hand. Don't waste what you've learned from a sales call by not taking the time to reflect afterward. Top performers understand the importance of reflecting after each call, and they take the time to assess what worked and what didn't after every customer interaction. Doing so better positions them to make the next call more efficient and more effective while better managing customer expectations.

4

A Solid Opening: Connect with Your Customers

A POOR OPENING is truly a lost opportunity—for you and your customer. A poor opening fails to lend your customer confidence in you, your company, and your product or service. It might lead your prospect to disengage or, even worse, to end the sales call altogether.

Being prepared for a compelling opening is a critical step to get your opening right. What happens when you pick up the phone to call a prospect without a plan? How well does just winging it work? How much are you able to accomplish with a poorly planned opening?

Chances are that winging it rarely (if ever) goes very well and that you don't accomplish as much as you might like when you launch into a sales call without a plan. The fact is that sales professionals who open calls without a plan are less successful than those who do plan. Furthermore, our research also tells us that an effective opening is one of the most undervalued phases of the sales process.

When are able to start the interaction with a solid opening, everything else falls naturally into place. A good opening gives you confidence, and it makes your customer feel comfortable. It sets the stage for the interaction and helps build positive momentum toward connecting with your customer. But solid openings don't happen by chance. They take planning and practice. The good news is that there are some specific steps you can take to ensure that you've mastered this critical selling skill so that you are prepared to deliver a solid opening every time and can tackle each opening with confidence.

Plan Your Opening

A good opening creates positive momentum that enables you to set the stage for the customer interaction, creating a connection and building rapport. Opening well requires sales professionals to blend planning with the art of being personable and the science of establishing a legitimate purpose for the sales call. We're not talking hours of planning or a long-winded monologue when it comes to opening well. Just a few minutes—and a few critical skills—can make all the difference in the world.

Planning the opening requires you to think about your customer, whether it's a new prospect or someone you've dealt with numerous times. As we discussed in Chapter 3, planning is critical during each phase of the sales cycle. Planning for a good opening means that you need to consider your customer, his organization, and his needs. It means you have to remember that your customer likely has a fair amount of information at his fingertips, and that he's done his research. With that, it's also important to think about what resistance you might face and the information you plan on sharing. The precall planner form we looked at in the last chapter (refer again to Figure 3.2) is a perfect tool to prepare you for a solid opening.

Opening well helps position you to become a trusted advisor to your customer. Think about what you're going to say to the customer and how you're going to say it. Think about those first few words that will come out of your mouth. Too often, sales professionals rush through this phase of the process, just launching in to their shtick, regardless of whether the prospect is ready for the discussion or even interested in what you have to say. Too many sales professionals just start the sales process without telling customers why they're calling, how the interaction will unfold, or what's in it for them.

Top-performing sales professionals understand that the opening sets the tone for the entire sales interaction. The opening might be quick—just a small portion of the overall time spent with a customer during the entire sales process—but that doesn't mean it's not important. In fact, it's vital for sales professionals to open well. Doing so requires four critical skills: mastering the greeting, creating connections, delivering a Legitimate Purpose Statement, and confirming.

Master the Greeting

The way in which you initially open a call with a customer is vital. That greeting, whether in your first meeting or your tenth, is your chance to get the conversation started in a positive way. And now that customers are busier than ever, sales professionals need to make the most of each moment they spend with their customers.

The actual opening—that first minute or two of each conversation—should be more than just a quick hello and some casual banter. A solid opening is both intentional and flexible. That means you have to open with confidence in your voice and your demeanor. A firm handshake, good eye contact, a warm smile, and relaxed body language will help your customer feel comfortable.

Remember that people respond in kind. So, if you open your call with intention and confidence, your customer will know it. If, on the other hand, you come at this critical step feeling uncertain, your customer will know that, too. For a solid opening, you have to put on your game face. Put yourself in the right place emotionally and mentally (a positive mindset is crucial here) so that you can give your customer your best.

Demonstrate confidence and show genuine enthusiasm for your organization and your product or service. Make it clear that you're looking forward to working with this customer and that you're excited about the prospect of helping her find solutions to whatever issues she and her company might have. Let her know that you've planned for the call by doing a little research into her and her organization.

Setting the tone in the first few minutes of your opening also requires that you be in tune with your customer. Pay attention to how she responds and mirror that behavior. Don't force a boisterous atmosphere during the meeting if the customer is clearly more subdued. Be flexible in your approach and remember that confidence isn't just about projecting your personality—it's also about being able to quickly recognize and adapt to your customer's style. Top-performing sales professionals who understand this, and who make the most of each opening, are in a better position to build the kind of rapport that allows them to be viewed as trusted advisors with their customers.

Create Connections

Building rapport and creating connections is critical when it comes to accelerating the sales process and closing more deals. A lot of people think they're really good at this, but it's easy to fall into some traps when it comes to creating connections.

Top-performing sales professionals understand that building rapport goes beyond making friendly banter. Don't assume that because your customer is friendly or personable or pleasant that you've built rapport. Rapport is built over time, and it takes constant work—as with any relationship.

Top performers also understand that rapport need not be extraordinarily personal or built on common interests that go far beyond the industry, product, or service that you and your customer are discussing. Chatting about the fact that you both have middle school students who play soccer might be one way to build rapport, but there are plenty of other approaches that allow you to maintain that balance between professional and personable.

Of course, there's some nuance here. Building good rapport is as much art as it is science, and it doesn't happen by chance. Try too hard, and it feels forced, transparent, or obvious. Overly perky banter can feel too salesy. There are much better ways to create connections.

Critical Moment: Understand Your Customer's Style

Building rapport can't be forced. Top-performing sales professionals understand the need to be flexible and adapt to the customer. They take the time to assess each customer's unique communication style and then adjust and adapt to that style in order to make the customer feel comfortable.

Each customer is unique, and how you go about building rapport will vary from customer to customer. Understanding these four general customer styles will help provide some guidance for effectively communicating with your customers.

- **Friendly and Personable.** This type of customer tends to be outgoing and full of energy. He might initiate chitchat during your conversations. When dealing with friendly, personable customers, match your energy level to theirs. Be sure to have ideas in mind for conversation, and take notice of issues or interests that frequently pop up.
- **Business-Oriented.** Customers who are all business typically limit banter, preferring to get straight to the issue at hand. Their tone of voice is often neutral or professional. When building rapport with business-oriented customers, be well prepared to discuss professional topics. Keep your energy level in check, and watch for signs that the customer is no longer interested in small talk.
- **Visionary.** Visionaries are usually enthusiastic and talkative and tend to gravitate toward creative ideas and concepts. It is important to maintain positive energy and be prepared to engage in fun or lively conversation when prompted. It's also important to stay focused on the big picture rather than providing too many details. Allow extra time to listen to the interests and opinions of this customer.
- **Cautious and Skeptical.** A serious tone often marks the cautious, skeptical customer. She might limit chitchat or test you by tossing out an objection or a challenging

(continued)

(*continued*)

question. It's important to stay calm, neutral, and professional with this customer. Allow time for the customer to think about what you are saying and offer guidance to assist her in drawing conclusions when needed.

Of course, most customers don't sit squarely in just one category. The key is to be versatile and flexible. Understanding these four customer styles will help you adapt and adjust as necessary, matching a customer's style so you can more readily put her at ease and more quickly build rapport.

Again, this is where planning comes in. A little advance research can go a long way in creating connections with customers. For example, if you're meeting with a partner in an accounting firm, your research might reveal that she's just written a white paper about value formulas. Better to talk about that than stumbling around trying to find some commonalities around your personal lives that you can chat about. Rather than risking attempts at personal conversations that might misfire, use the opportunity to demonstrate that you took the time to do some research and plan for the call.

Note that this kind of conversation can serve as an advantage for you, not just in the fact that it helps build rapport but also because it likely will differentiate you from other sales professionals who are trying to make connections solely on a personal level. In demonstrating that you've planned the opening, that you've researched the customer, and that you're able to converse about things that are important to her, you're able to add value to the relationship right away.

Professional rapport should be carefully crafted and cultivated over time. Planning how you will open each and every sales call with each and every customer will make it evident that you've done your homework. It's just one simple but critical step in gathering the seeds that can be planted throughout various conversations you'll have with your customers—seeds that will help grow your relationships over time.

Critical Moment: Use Research to Create Connections

Building rapport is the foundation of creating lasting connections with your customers. Learning key information about your customers in advance of each sales call will put you in good stead to have the kind of conversations that make your customers feel comfortable while making it clear that you've done your homework—and that you're interested in them.

Instead of struggling to find common ground among the many and varied personal interests customers might have, top-performing sales reps understand the value of finding areas in the professional spectrum that will allow them to build rapport.

These areas can include past companies the customer has worked for, areas of professional expertise, past colleges or universities attended, professional affiliations or organizations to which the customer belongs, articles or papers he's written, boards he might sit on, and even charitable or philanthropic organizations for which he volunteers.

Sources for such information include LinkedIn and other social media, the customer's company website, blogs or columns, alumni associations, and so on.

Building rapport along professional lines differentiates you from the many sales reps who chat up prospects using tired personal lines of conversation—children, family, and sports, for example. That doesn't mean you can't bring some personal aspects into the conversation. But doing research into the customer's professional background and planning ahead for each sales call will provide you another avenue through which to create connections while adding value to the conversation.

Deliver a Legitimate Purpose Statement

As you move deeper into the opening, it's essential to make clear to your customer why you are talking with him. After you've worked through a greeting and started to create a connection with your customer, it's time to deliver what we call a Legitimate Purpose Statement.

The LPS is an important part of the opening to get right. This is a critical skill, and it might seem simple on the surface, but executing it well is more difficult than you might think at first blush.

In this part of the call, you want to let your customer know the purpose of the conversation. Letting your customer know why you're calling establishes the framework for the call. This serves not only as your guide for what you want to accomplish during the call but also as a road map for your customer so he, too, knows what to expect. It's simple enough: state your purpose.

The trickier part of the LPS is ensuring that the purpose statement is legitimate. To make the purpose statement legitimate, you have to let the customer know what's in it for him. Why should he spend time with you on the call? Remember: the call isn't just about what you want to accomplish. You also have to let the customer know why he should spend time with you. You have to articulate the value for him.

By delivering a Legitimate Purpose Statement—instead of just diving in with your usual shtick or jumping straight to the discovering phase of the sales process—you are building trust and instilling confidence because you've given the customer the opportunity to hear and digest the "why" behind your call. Doing this will help you achieve buy-in, which will make the call more productive for both of you.

The LPS also helps you to avoid making pointless sales calls. Because you have to think about why you're calling the customer and because you have to plan what you're going to say, you avoid those rambling calls that go nowhere because your purpose isn't clear. This is especially true with follow-up calls.

We aren't big fans of the follow-up call placed just for the purpose of following up. In fact, one of the worst things a sales rep can do is check in just to follow up or touch base. Why? Because there's really no purpose to these calls and certainly no value to the customer. Generic, touching-base, follow-up calls aren't focused on the customer. They're all about the sales rep. Touching base just for the sake of checking in isn't productive. In fact, this call can actually backfire, costing you credibility because it provides no value to the customer and likely feels to him like an intrusive waste of time. That can shift momentum out of your favor, which isn't at all what you want.

If you're reaching out to a customer, you need to have a legitimate purpose, and you need to be able to articulate what's in it for the customer. If you don't have that, you should reconsider why you're calling that customer in the first place.

Each call needs to provide clear value to the customer. It has to advance the sales process. If it doesn't, it provides zero value—to your customer or to you. Even worse, it can result in the dreaded "let me get back to you" line from your customer, which can lead to a higher likelihood of stalled deals.

Instead of calling just to follow up or check in or touch base, deliver a straightforward LPS in a confident, concise manner:

- "As you may know, we help businesses such as yours [do this], and have been able to achieve [X] results. I'd like to spend a few minutes learning about your operations so I can provide you with the information you are looking for."
- "Today I'd like to better understand your needs and requirements. Once I learn more about what's most important to you and your organization, I can provide a few recommendations for you."

Top-performing sales professionals know how to articulate the reason for and direction of each call in a way that makes it clear that the conversation will be of value to the customer. They know how to deliver a strong LPS that is authentic and organic without feeling staged or rehearsed. At the beginning of each sales interaction, top performers establish what they want to cover, and they get feedback from the customer regarding that agenda. They do so by confirming with their customer at every step of the conversation, which is another key aspect of a solid opening.

Critical Moment: Connect with Presence

Connecting with your customers requires you to communicate with them, and how you do that requires you to use three elements: words, vocal quality, and body language. Together these make up your presence.

What you say, how you say it, and your manner while saying it together convey your message to your customers. When choosing words, consider your customers' style (discussed above). Speak their language—figuratively and literally. Use the same key terms and phrases they use. For example, if a customer keeps saying she needs to "get buy-in" from her team before moving ahead, don't rephrase and ask what she needs to get her team "on board" instead. Mirror your customer's words. Doing so makes it clear that you're paying attention, and that goes a long way in making your customer feel comfortable.

The same goes for your vocal quality. Tone, speed, diction, inflection—all of these affect your presence. You can use your vocal qualities to set a positive tone for each meeting with your customer. Remember that how you say it is just as important—if not more so—as what you say.

Body language also conveys meaning. Your appearance, your handshake, your smile, your posture—all of that speaks volumes about your professionalism and how engaged you are with your customer.

Top-performing sales reps are aware of their own presence, and they strive to modify their presence in order to accommodate different customer styles. You can do this, too:

- **Allow for More Pauses in Your Speech.** If it seems as though your customer needs more time to digest the information you're sharing or to answer questions you raise, take a moment to let her reflect before continuing with the conversation.

■ **Mirror Your Customer's Body Language.** It can be useful to align your body language with your customer's, but make sure your presence remains positive. Lean forward when she does, but think twice about crossing your arms, for instance, which might inadvertently convey a negative tone.

■ **Modify Your Energy Level and Tone of Voice.** Make sure your energy and tone is in sync with your customer's. For instance, be succinct and provide only the most relevant information to a customer who has a strong business style.

Two different people could say exactly the same thing, word for word, but have their message received differently, all because of the other aspects of presence—vocal quality and body language. Think about what your presence says about you. Think, too, about what your customer's presence says about her. And make sure you're speaking the same language.

Confirm for Feedback

Delivering an effective LPS is a critical component of a solid opening. But that doesn't mean you should just tell your customer what you want to talk about and then forge ahead with the conversation. You have to make sure your customer understands what the call is about and how it will be of value to him, and you also have to make sure that you're in sync with each other.

Top-performing sales reps take the time to make sure that the LPS they articulate to their customers is aligned with what their customers actually want to talk about. They understand that by preparing a discussion about X when the customer really wants to discuss Y, they run the risk of losing serious credibility.

The key here is simple but effective: confirm with your customer what you will discuss. Asking a simple question after you deliver your LPS is all it takes:

- "How does that sound?" or
- "Does that sound good?" or
- "Does that cover everything you'd like to discuss?" or
- "Will that work for you?"

This might seem really simple or even overly basic, but our research tells us that this tiny but critical step is one of the most powerful—yet overlooked—facets of an effective sales call. Many sales reps fail to confirm that their customers understand the purpose for the call, how it will be of value to them, and that they're on board with the LPS. Too many sales reps don't stop to bring the customer back into the conversation. Instead, they just push on through, assuming the customer is tagging along.

This is a mistake.

Sales reps skip this step for any number of reasons (none of them good). They might fear losing control of the conversation. They might fear what could happen if the customer, in fact, is not on board with the LPS. They might fear having to field an early objection that they're not ready to deal with. They might think they know better, operating under the common misconception that they know both what the customer needs and what the best way to go about meeting those needs is.

This kind of reasoning will get you nowhere fast. Top-performing sales professionals confidently and concisely deliver a strong Legitimate Purpose Statement, and then—right away—confirm with the customer that he's on board. And if he's not on board, it provides the sales rep an opportunity to incorporate the customer's own thoughts as to how the conversation should go.

For instance, the customer might say, "Yes, that sounds good. Let's talk." Or he might say, "That sounds okay, but I also want to find out about how your team supports implementation."

Right there is an opportunity for you to hear your customer, assess his needs, and tailor your LPS to meet those needs. By listening to your customer and adjusting your LPS as necessary, you not only make the call more productive but also further build rapport by showing your customer that you're taking his needs into consideration. So, if the customer does provide the kind of feedback that makes you rethink your LPS, be sure to reposition your approach accordingly and then reconfirm.

Confirming isn't something that happens just once or only during the opening phase of the sales process or only with new prospects. Top-performing sales reps do this at a few key moments throughout the sales process, and they do so with every customer. In fact, confirming is such an important tool that it is incorporated throughout the Critical Selling framework.

How does that sound?

Critical Moment: Use the LPS in E-Mail and Voice Mail

Delivering a strong LPS when calling on a customer, whether in person or by phone, is an effective way to ensure that you're communicating well with your customer in a targeted, concise way and that you're providing clear value to the customer. Doing so helps build rapport, makes each sales call more productive, and provides the momentum to keep the sales cycle moving forward.

Of course, you can't always contact your customer right when you want to. Sometimes you have to leave a message. In those cases, whether using e-mail or voice mail, you should use the Legitimate Purpose Statement as a primary component of your communication. These in-between messages can go a long way in keeping the conversation going, if they are effective.

There's a simple formula for leveraging an LPS in messages: your name + LPS + follow-up steps + contact details = best practice in using LPS.

The e-mail message might sound similar to this:

Good afternoon, Justin,

    I hope this message finds you well. I'm reaching out about our discussion last week. As you may recall, you had asked for information about the two versions of Product X so you could

(continued)

(*continued*)

> *share the details with your team. You also wanted to know more about implementation processes. I have the information you requested and would like to set up a call to discuss. Would Monday afternoon or Tuesday morning work for a call? Please let me know some dates and times that would work best for you. You can reach me at sarak@email.com or 800-XXX-XXXX. I look forward to hearing from you.*
>
> *Thanks!*
>
> *Sara*

Close the Opening with Some Reflection

When you think about all the things you need to do well during those first few minutes of conversation with your customer, you realize that there's actually a lot going on. What the impact of those first few minutes is on your customer depends on how well you plan the call, master the greeting, create connections, deliver a Legitimate Purpose Statement, and confirm that your customer is on board.

If you get the opening right, the rest of the call—and the rest of the sales process—will fall naturally into place, building on positive momentum. If you get it wrong, though, the effect will be detrimental (and possibly even ruinous) to the rest of the sales process.

How will you know if you get it right? By listening to your customer, getting his feedback, and confirming. Top-performing sales professionals go one step further: they reflect.

Remember our discussion in Chapter 3 about the importance of planning and reflecting. Don't waste all the work you've done by planning a good opening, getting feedback from your customer, and confirming with him by just ending the meeting and moving on to the next item on your to-do list. Think about how the call went.

What worked well? What didn't work? What key takeaways did you get from your customer? What kind of follow-up work do you need to do? What do you next need to provide to your customer in order to move the process forward?

Remember that the process is always about the customer. Think of it not just as a sales process but as a customer-buying process: How can you best move the customer from one step to the next? Connecting with the customer and building a lasting relationship are what matters most at this point.

A solid opening is a critical step in the sales process. It not only opens the door but also provides you the opportunity to learn more about your customer, his needs, and how you can meet those needs. That kind of feedback is priceless.

Thinking about the feedback your customer gave you will put you in good stead when it comes to asking the kind of questions that help move the process forward. Asking the right questions at the right time is critical when it comes to creating connections with your customer. The answers you glean will allow you to discover more about your customer's needs, which is another critical step in the process. We'll discuss that next, in Chapter 5.

Critical Selling: Lessons Learned

- A poor opening is a lost opportunity that can hurt your credibility with your customer. A solid opening, though, helps everything else to fall naturally into place.
- Planning for a solid opening requires you to think about your customer, his organization, and their needs. It means you have to think about what you're going to say and how you're going to say it. And it means you have to blend planning with the art of being personable and the science of delivering a Legitimate Purpose Statement.
- Top-performing sales reps don't underestimate the simple power of a well-delivered Legitimate Purpose Statement. They make sure to state each LPS clearly, concisely, and confidently.

- Confirm and reflect. Top performers understand that confirming is important to ensure that the customer is on board and that they are aligned. Reflecting enables you to look back on how things went and how you might be able to improve the next time.

5

It's All about Discovering: Get to Know Your Customers

Discovering needs is one of those things that just about every sales rep says he does. But the truth is that there is a large disparity between top-performing sales professionals who really do a good job of discovering needs and who understand the value of doing so and sales reps who might ask a few basic questions before jumping into their presentations.

Discovering your customers' needs is critical because those needs drive buying opportunities. As discussed in Chapter 4, a good opening sets the stage for you to get to know your customer and discover his needs. Those needs are what create the motivation, purpose, and decision-making impetus behind your customer's drive to move forward in finding solutions with you. Good sales reps ask questions to uncover information that validates needs for the solutions they can provide. Top-performing sales reps, however, dig deeper to discover the root cause of their customers' needs and then utilize that information to more clearly demonstrate how their products, services, and solutions meet those needs.

There's an important difference here. Asking questions to confirm that your customers' known needs fit with the product or service you sell is a lot different than discovering needs at a deeper level and uncovering those needs that even your customers may not be aware of. Top performers focus on the latter approach, asking questions and actively listening to the answers in order to discover all they can about their customers and their needs, goals, and expectations.

Sales is all about discovering. Many salespeople associate selling with presenting information and closing deals, but the reality is that most selling occurs during the discovering phase of the process. By asking questions, listening to the answers, and discovering needs, you are able to stimulate interest, build trust, earn credibility, meet customers where they are in the buying process, and separate yourself from the competition.

Our research shows that top performers spend more time in this stage of the sales process than in any other stage. They understand that time invested in discovering actually accelerates the sales process. Unfortunately, many salespeople look at this in the completely opposite way. In fact, our research tells us that lower performers spend more time presenting, overcoming objections, and closing (or attempting to close) in the mistaken belief that doing so will help them secure the sale more quickly. But the truth is that skipping the discovering phase, or giving it the short shrift, actually lengthens the sales process—nor does it win you any bonus points when it comes to earning trust.

We have found that if you ask the right questions and listen to what your customers say, they'll tell you exactly what their needs are and what they require to meet those needs. Really communicating with your customers by asking questions and listening to the responses helps create win-win solutions that allow you to become a trusted advisor and build lasting relationships.

What's more is that our research isn't alone in these findings. University of Nebraska–Lincoln professors Susie Pryor and Avinash

Malshe recently found that "[c]ommunication skills are the single most important determinant of effectiveness in both sales and sales management."[1] We couldn't agree more. By understanding what matters most to your customers, you can tailor solutions to meet those needs. And once you do that, you can accelerate the sales process and close more deals, all while differentiating yourself from the competition.

Understand the Benefits of Discovering

Just about everyone who works in sales, sales management, and sales training extols the virtues of discovering needs. Even so, it's one of those skills that too many sales professionals skim over on the way to presenting solutions. This is a mistake, because the benefits of doing well here can mean the difference between simply taking an order and consistently closing better deals with customers with whom you've built lasting relationships.

Doing well in the discovering phase of the sales process is critical. It requires you to ask the right questions and actively listen to the answers. We'll talk about that in the pages that follow. But in order to understand how to do this well, you should first understand why you should do it.

Taking full advantage of the discovering phase helps you uncover quality information. It helps you build a long-term relationship with your customer. And it helps you differentiate yourself from the competition. These are no small things.

We have found that if you ask the right questions, your customers more often than not will tell you both what to sell to them and how to sell to them. Of course, asking questions also helps you discover the kinds of details about your customer, his needs, and his organization that will help you make a winning presentation, build a quote, draft a proposal, and so on. Asking questions during the discovering phase will help you uncover quality information that reveals the details you need to help meet your customer's needs. But that's not even the half of it.

Top-performing sales professionals understand that asking great questions not only uncovers quality information, but that doing so also strongly influences how your customers perceive you and, therefore, the relationship they have with you. Sales reps who fail to ask good questions during the discovering phase are typically seen as little more than order takers—which is not at all how you want your customers to view you.

One of the easiest ways to move from order taker to trusted advisor is by asking thoughtful questions designed to get your customers to open up and think differently about their particular situation. Top performers focus more on asking questions than on regurgitating information about how great they, their organization, and their products and services are. Because of that, top performers more quickly and more effectively build credibility. When customers understand that your intention is to understand their needs rather than to sell them a widget, it puts them at ease. That in turn makes them more willing to open up and provide the quality information you need in order to provide them with the best solution possible. It becomes a virtuous circle: the more comfortable a customer feels, the more he opens up; the more he opens up, the better quality information you get; the better information you get, the better you can meet his needs; the more he perceives that you want to discover those needs, the stronger your relationship will be. In the end, asking questions and eliciting quality information helps build the kind of credibility that not only helps you meet your customer's needs but also accelerates the sales process and leads to closing more deals.

In a day and age when differentiating yourself on product or service is more and more difficult, it's a mistake to try to use the same old approach to sell the same stuff that everyone else is selling. Your approach is critical, and making the most of the discovering phase is a key way to differentiate yourself from the competition. By asking really great questions, offering ideas, and fully exploring the situation, you can show your customer not only that you are knowledgeable but also that you are a helpful resource. That you're more than just a salesperson.

This is especially true when considering both known and unknown needs. All customers have needs, but only some know precisely what they are. Many customers have yet to realize the extent of their needs. Top-performing sales professionals make the most of the discovering phase to ask thoughtful questions that explore the customer's full range of needs, oftentimes helping customers uncover needs they didn't even know they had. This is one of the strongest ways top performers differentiate themselves, providing value and ideas to the customer not through products or services but through their approach.

Ask the Right Questions

Questioning enables you to gather the necessary information to understand your customer's unique situation. This is the foundation of a customer-focused approach. You need to understand the customer, his needs, his priorities, and so on. Our research shows that the role of and the importance of a customer-focused sales approach has evolved over the years. In fact, as we discussed in Chapter 1, there are two critical changes in particular: your customers know more and are at different points in their buying journeys. Therefore, you, as a sales professional, have to focus on their needs and find out where each customer is in the buying process in order to adapt and meet them where they are. That requires you to not only ask some questions but also to ask the right questions.

The notion of asking questions, of course, isn't new. Most people would agree that if you want to sell something to your customer, you have to ask him at least a few questions. Unfortunately, however, most people aren't very good at this critical skill.

It's important to build a solid understanding of your customer's needs by exploring key areas of focus and by asking targeted questions that will allow you to fully understand your customer, his organization, their particular situation, and their needs. It's also critical that you do so in a conscious manner—meaning that you ask targeted, focused questions that will allow you to dig deep in order to discover crucial information about your customer. It's not just about asking a bunch of questions to get your customer to open up. It's about asking the right questions in the right way at the right time.

This can be harder than it seems. Why? Because asking the right questions in the right way at the right time requires that you not only ask the right questions but also actively listen to the answers. It's critical to hear not only what your customer is saying but also what he's not saying. It's also important to pay attention to vocal qualities and body language (we'll look at this later in the chapter).

More often than not, asking the right questions during the discovering phase requires a little finesse when it comes to phrasing your questions. Beginning with questions that are more open-ended in nature can be quite helpful. Such questions are designed to open the floodgates so that your customer can really think about his situation and his needs. You can get your customer thinking with questions such as these:

- How would you describe your current situation?
- What does your ideal situation look like?
- What would it take to get to your ideal situation?
- What strategies have worked best for you in the past?
- What has kept you from achieving your goals and objectives faster?
- What are some of the biggest challenges facing you right now?
- What elements of your current product or service do you like best?
- What elements do you like least?
- What is the single most important action that could transform your company?
- What would keep you from moving forward?

Above all, it's critical to keep in mind that the discovering phase should be a conversation. It's a two-way communication designed to provide an avenue for your customer not only to share what he thinks he needs but also to explore other uncovered or unmet needs—not so you can push your own agenda but so that you can work together to find the right solution for him. That might be a solution he's never even thought of.

Critical Moment: Phrase Questions to Uncover Top-Quality Information

How we phrase questions is just as important as asking questions in the first place. Whether questions are closed-ended (i.e., questions that typically result in yes or no answers) or open-ended (i.e., questions that prompt expanded answers) can dramatically affect the type and amount of information you glean from your customer.

There's some skill involved here. Think about the best interviewers—Oprah Winfrey, Barbara Walters, and Larry King, for example—and how they phrase questions in just the right way at just the right time in order to get someone to open up. We're not saying your questioning should bring your customers to tears or heartfelt confessions, but you do want to ask the kind of questions that go beyond "How can I help you today?"

Phrasing questions in the right way can help you elicit quality information that helps you uncover your customer's needs. But even more than that, asking the right questions in the right way at the right time can help you uncover not only what the customer thinks he needs but also myriad possibilities the customer might never have even thought of. Questioning can help you dig deeper, allowing your customer to think beyond what must be done or what should be done to what could be done.

We think of this as "strategic questioning," and there is definitely an art to this. It is important not only to ask thoughtful questions designed to elicit critical information

(continued)

(*continued*)

but also to show legitimate interest. Customers can easily tell when you are being disingenuous, so it's important to be sincere and authentic. The key isn't to ask questions designed with an agenda but to ask questions that will prompt the customer to think more deeply, to think in a new way about his situation and what could be done to improve it.

Strategic questions should prompt the customer to think about:

- Information about his current situation, including the solution he's using now
- Attitudes and opinions about the current state, current provider, available options, competitors, and so on.
- Expectations and perspectives about possible solutions
- Possible actions for meeting needs

Top performers aren't afraid to dig deep—or to help their customers think more holistically about their current situation and potential solutions. They aren't afraid to ask why. They aren't afraid to say, "Tell me more about that." And safe in the knowledge that, together, they can find solutions to even their most nagging problems, they are not afraid to guide their customers toward the unknown.

Dig Deep to Uncover Unknowns

In our observation, many sales reps are hesitant and at times even afraid to dig deep when it comes to asking the right questions. As a result, they ask questions that only scratch the surface, thus running the risk of asking the same questions that every other sales rep asks and not differentiating themselves. This is a missed opportunity.

Top performers understand that asking the right questions requires them to go beyond the obvious. Discovering isn't about asking surface-level questions. Unfortunately, however, these are just the issues that most sales reps focus on, with simple questions such as:

- How many widgets do you need?
- What should the setup be?
- What are you looking for?
- What's your time frame or deadline?
- How can we help you with that?

Not only are these questions basic but they're nothing that will differentiate you from the competition. Every sales rep out there is asking these same questions. Your job as a top performer is to dig deeper.

To do that, you have to ask the follow-up questions. You have to listen to what your customer is saying—and to what he's not saying. You have to seek to uncover not only what the customer needs (or thinks he needs) but also the circumstances that are driving that need. What's really behind the need? Why does it exist? What factors are affecting the situation? Why is it important to meet this need right now? What's in it for the customer and his organization? What will happen if the need isn't met?

Beyond these follow-up questions, you can dig even deeper. For how long has this situation existed? What challenges has the customer faced in meeting this need? What other solutions have been tried? In what ways have other solutions failed or succeeded?

Explore, too, the decision-making factors involved in the situation. Ask your customer who is involved in the decision-making process. Ask what his expectations are—and whether they are in sync with those of the rest of his team.

If you're able to ask the right questions, you can get your customers to think differently. You can get them to think beyond the surface, beyond the details they are consciously aware of, to information that might be unknown even to them. This is the real nugget. If you can get your customer to think, to really open up, it's quite possible through targeted questioning that he'll come to a realization he hadn't thought of before—one that you can help him with.

Targeted questioning will enable you to gather necessary information that will help you understand your customer's unique situation. We understand that asking the right questions at the right time in the right way can be overwhelming. It takes practice. You might not know where to start. We can help with that. Our research has uncovered six critical areas of focus that all salespeople should explore with their customers, and these are an excellent place to start.

Target the Six Critical Areas of Focus

Top-performing sales professionals understand that asking good questions helps increase their understanding of their customers' needs. Doing so puts them in the best position possible to tailor solutions that benefit their customers in valuable ways.

Our research has uncovered six critical areas of focus (see Figure 5.1) that help sales reps build a solid understanding of their customers:

- Customer situation
- Customer needs and challenges
- People and relationships
- Buying process
- Options and alternatives
- Impact

These six critical areas of focus need to be explored so that you're ready to move on to the next step in the process. Top-performing sales reps understand that addressing these areas of focus will help them gather quality data from their customers as quickly and

Figure 5.1   **Six Critical Areas of Focus**

efficiently as possible. Addressing these areas of focus should be done in a conversational, fluid manner. This might happen during one conversation; it might take place over several conversations. It depends on the nature of the transaction, the complexity of the sale, and the customer's situation. So with that, let's look at each of the six critical areas of focus.

Customer Situation

Assessing the customer's current situation is usually the first issue to be addressed in the sales interaction. In this area of focus, you want to understand the customer's current state (i.e., what currently exists in the customer's environment) and the customer's level of satisfaction (i.e., how happy the customer is with the current state).

For many sales reps, assessing the customer's situation is typically the easiest part of the discovering stage. Asking questions such as, "What products or services are you currently using?" or "How satisfied are you with your current product or service?" is fundamental stuff. But top-performing sales professionals use open-ended questions and a conversational approach to dig a little deeper, asking questions or using statements such as, "Tell me more about the current product or service you are using," and "What aspects of your current product are working best for you?" and "Where would you like to see improvements in the product you're currently using?" Questions such as these can help open the door to discover high-quality information from your customer that will allow you to better tailor a solution to his needs. Drawing out additional details helps provide more clues about the customer so that you can best discern his current situation.

It's important here not to rush the process. Don't speed through your list of questions as though you're merely on a time-sensitive fact-finding mission. It's not an interrogation; it's a conversation. So, ask open-ended questions. Listen to your customer's answers—not just what he says, but how he says it. Circle back with follow-up questions that not only show that you've been listening, but that you earnestly want to understand the customer and his needs.

Customer Needs and Challenges

Just as gauging the customer's situation has for many sales reps become second nature, so too is discerning needs and challenges fairly common in sales today. Although most sales professionals do this to some extent, it's easy to fall short on how deep you can delve into this area.

This critical area of focus is one of the most important because it is here where you begin to truly understand your customer's needs as well as what is of top importance in his mind. In identifying customer needs and challenges, you want to find out what the customer wants to achieve, what he wants to improve, what his current problems are, and what factors are contributing to those problems. In this critical area, you want to focus on:

- Needs and opportunities
- Problems and challenges

- The customer's motivation to act
- The customer's priorities

By asking the right questions, you provide the customer with an opportunity to explain his situation and perhaps air some grievances about his current situation. It's also an opportunity for you to gather more quality data that you can use to tailor a solution that meets his needs and priorities.

Here again, top-performing sales reps go a little deeper. Ask the customer what the ideal situation, product, or service would feature. Ask him what the perfect solution would entail.

Good sales reps frequently ask about needs, opportunities, problems, and challenges—that's often part of the customer-focused selling approach. But top-performing sales professionals can gather even more information by asking the customer why it's important to him to explore new options right now. Top performers ask questions such as, "What drove you to explore options with us today?" and "Could you give me a sense of why this is important to you and your team right now?" They also use the conversation to gain insight into priorities, asking open-ended questions such as, "Which of the concerns you've mentioned are most important to you?" and "Of everything we've discussed today, what is most important to you?"

By asking your customer what's driving his decision, you can gather additional information that will allow you to present your product or service in a uniquely tailored way that is specific to your customer.

People and Relationships

Selling is about building lasting relationships with your customers, who look to you as a trusted advisor. During the discovering phase, it's critical to find out everything you can about the people and the relationships involved in the buying decision. Research shows that one of the biggest changes in customer buying behavior is that more people are involved in the decision-making process. Therefore, focusing on people and relationships is more important now than ever before.

Top-performing sales reps find out key information about their contact and his team, such as who is involved in the sales process, what their roles are, and what individual needs must be considered. They do this by asking questions such as, "Who would you say is your strongest advocate in your organization? How does that individual affect the buying decision?" and "Who in the organization has the most influence on the buying decision?" and "Who do you think will need some additional time and attention in order to support the buying decision?"

How deeply you dive into the people and relationships that affect your customer will depend on a variety of factors, including the complexity of the sale, the structure of the customer's organization, the individuals involved in the buying decision, and so forth. The key here is to focus on the interactions and relationships that will have an impact on the sale.

Buying Process

As you think about the people and relationships that will affect the sale, so too must you consider the customer's buying process. Find out what you can about stages in the buying cycle along with the customer's decision-making process, budget, schedule, lead time, and so forth. Focus not only on the part of the process in which you're involved but also on the customer's entire process. Ask questions about how frequently the customer places orders, what his organization's decision-making process looks like, how often his organization typically replaces inventory, and how procurement might play a role in the decision. Questions along these lines can be simple and direct, such as, "How frequently do you replenish inventory?" and "At what point does procurement get involved in the process?" and "What additional steps do you need to take before a decision is made?"

By understanding how the customer and his organization typically operate, you'll be in a better position to ensure that you can best support the customer in his decision-making process by engaging in the right way at the right time.

Options and Alternatives

In a day and age when customers are both savvier and busier, you can count on the fact that your customer has done his research and that he likely is considering at least one other provider. Assume that he is looking at several options and alternatives, and ask some questions about what those might be. Don't be afraid to ask about the specific options the customer is considering and which he's leaning toward at this juncture. Ask about which other firms he's investigating and how he thinks the competition stacks up. Ask what he likes and dislikes about the options and alternatives that might fit his needs. Be sure to use open-ended questions such as "Which alternatives have you been investigating?" and "Which of the options that you've been exploring seem most attractive at this point?" and "What about the current options available to you do you find most compelling?"

Asking your customer some targeted questions about the options and alternatives he's considering will provide you keen insight into how you can best tailor a solution to meet his needs. It also will give you a window into how customers view your competition, which can be helpful intelligence when you look to present your solution in a way that is differentiated from your competition.

Impact

In addition to learning about your customer's needs, priorities, and options, it's important to find out what the impact of the buying decision will be for him and his organization. Buying a widget is never just about increasing the quantity of widgets—and selling a widget should never be just about getting more widgets into the hands of your customers.

Top-performing sales professionals understand that asking about the impact of the decision helps the customer consider what will or what could happen by taking action or leaving things as they are. They know to ask questions about both the benefits of change and the consequences of sticking with the status quo. They discuss with the customer what the impact would be if the new product improved efficiency or tightened up the supply chain. They ask the customer what kind of return on investment he's looking for and how his firm will measure that ROI.

Questioning and discovering in this critical area of focus might sound like "What will the impact on gross margins be if the product's fail rate is reduced by 3 percent in the manufacturing cycle?" or "If you were to lose your position as market leader for this technology, what impact might that have on meeting your quarterly targets?"

Gauging the impact of the buying decision on your customer and his organization is one of the critical skills that truly separate a top performer from the rest. There are many associated benefits in bringing up this topic with your customers. In asking questions in these areas—and by listening to the answers—you'll be better positioned to help your customers clearly see the value of your solution.

Asking the right questions at the right time and in the right way can take you far in terms of getting to know your customers and building long-term relationships with them. But you can't just ask the questions. You have to listen to the answers. You have to hear what your customers are saying.

Listen Actively to Understand Your Customer

Listening is one of those skills that is easier said than done. Active listening goes a lot deeper than most people think, and it's a critical skill for sales professionals. In fact, research shows that "listening may be the single most important skill that salespeople can possess."[2]

Listening goes beyond just hearing the words coming out of your customer's mouth. Listening is not something you do with just your ears. It's a thinking exercise that requires you to interpret what you are hearing and engage in follow-up questions so that you can make sure you understand what your customer is saying—and what she's thinking.

It's important to acknowledge that sometimes, what the customer says is different from what she really means—not because she's purposefully trying to be evasive, but because communicating effectively can be difficult. For these reasons, it's critical that you be dialed in to the conversation in order to decipher the information your customer is sharing with you, both verbally and nonverbally.

In fact, research shows that "[t]he most effective level of listening combines empathy with the techniques of active listening."[3] Furthermore, "customers' perceptions of the quality of salespeople's listening were found to be positively related to customers' trust in salespeople, their satisfaction with them, and their desire to do future business with them."[4]

Our research confirms the importance of active listening. Your customer wants to know that you're listening and that you're hearing her. She wants to know that you are being attentive, and she wants to see that you are actively involved in the conversation. If you don't appear to be engaged, you run the risk of losing credibility and shutting down the lines of communication with your customer. In fact, "a study of industrial salespeople found that one of the most important reasons that salespeople are unsuccessful is failure to listen."[5]

Just as consequential as the failure to listen is the perception that you're not listening. When conversing with your customer, it's important to maintain eye contact and acknowledge that she is sharing information. Don't bury your head in your notes while the customer is talking. Be sure to eliminate any potential distractions—and that includes silencing your cell phone and anything else that might pull your attention away from your customer. Little details can make a world of difference in the sales process, and it's important to show the customer that you are actively engaged in the conversation.

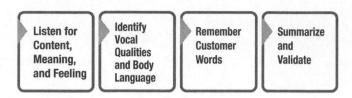

Figure 5.2 Four Steps to Active Listening

Pryor's and Malshe's recent research confirms this. "[A]ll listening is not equal," they write. "Buyers want not only evidence that the [salesperson] has heard and understood them, but that the [salesperson] has a genuine interest in the buyer. [Salespeople], then, have the opportunity to enhance relationships merely by signaling to the buyer not only are needs understood, but also that they matter."[6]

This is easier said than done. But there is a process that can help ensure you avoid the perception that you aren't listening, that you don't make assumptions about what you're hearing (or not hearing), and that you don't listen selectively, hearing only the information you want to hear. Figure 5.2 illustrates that process.

Actively listening requires that you listen not only for words or key phrases but also for content, meaning, and feeling. It means you need to pay attention to both vocal qualities and body language. It asks that you take note of the customer's words and phrasing and that you summarize what the customer has said and validate that you've really heard her. There's more to listening than just hearing words. In fact, there's a lot going on in active listening. So let's look at the process.

Listen for Content, Meaning, and Feeling

Subtext and context are critical items when it comes to listening to your customers. That means you have to listen for content, meaning, and feeling. You have to pay attention to the literal or actual language stated by the customer, the meaning or intent of the message as well as the feeling or emotion behind what is being said. Sales professionals who do this find that they are able to more quickly and accurately understand customer needs.

Listening for content, meaning, and feeling often means you have to slow down. Don't rush the conversation. Don't assume that you know what your customer is going to say or what her next sentence is going to lead to. It can be easy to start filtering some of what you hear, listening for key terms and phrases that will help you prove your point. Don't do it. Exceptional listeners don't make assumptions about what their customers will say. Instead, they are able to slow down; listen to what's being said (and not said); and focus on content, meaning, and feeling.

Of course, listening isn't just about what your customer says; it's also about the meaning and feeling behind it. Words mean one thing, but the way in which she conveys the message speaks to what she's saying more completely. Words that she repeats again and again also carry weight.

In actively listening to your customer for content, meaning, and feeling, you can discern not only those overt needs that she discusses directly with you but also those issues that might provide you with opportunities to further differentiate yourself as someone who takes the time and makes the effort to really hear what is important to her.

Identify Vocal Qualities and Body Language

One of the key differentiators between good sales professionals and top performers is the ability to identify what the customer is thinking, feeling, or expressing through her vocal qualities and body language. Top-performing sales reps are attuned to the customer's verbal and nonverbal cues throughout each conversation, picking up on clues that provide further insight into her needs and priorities.

Vocal qualities include things such as her tone, emphasis, inflection, and pace. This also means more subtle clues such as sighs or extended pauses. Body language includes such things as gestures, facial expressions, and other nonverbals. Don't assume you know what these verbal and nonverbal cues mean. Rather, consider them as clues to further discovering more about your customer.

For instance, when your customer starts talking about her supply chain and the kinks that she needs to smooth out in it, you might notice that her tone and facial expression becomes much more serious. You might say, for example, "It seems that this is really important to you. Can you tell me more about what you need in order to smooth out your supply chain?"

It's never safe to assume you know what your customer is thinking or feeling. But it is always safe to ask her what she's thinking and feeling. Don't be afraid to follow up on vocal and body language cues; doing so provides further opportunity for you to discover more about her needs and priorities. For example, it can be easy to assume that a customer who displays crossed arms and crossed legs is closed-minded, annoyed, or frustrated. Or it might just be that she's cold and wishes you would turn up the heat (literally, not figuratively).

Eye contact, nods, shrugs, smiles, posture . . . body language can come in many forms. For instance, if your customer is relentlessly tapping her pen on her desk, take notice. During a break in the conversation, find a way to ask about it. A little nudge such as "How are we on time?" might address what appears to be impatience of some kind.

Remember Customer Words

Moving along in the process of actively listening, we come to the importance of remembering—and repeating—customer words. As you converse with your customer, listen for words, terms, and key phrases that she repeats. Pay attention to the lingo she uses when describing her needs and her organization. Take note of the jargon that pops up in her speech. She's using those words—those particular words—for a reason.

Customer words are those words, terms, and phrases that a customer continually uses to describe a need, problem, or challenge.

In repeating them (likely in an unconscious manner), your customer is conveying to you their importance, and in doing that, she is telling you what her needs and priorities are.

An easy way to differentiate yourself from the competition is to take note of those words, remember them, and incorporate her words into the conversation. Doing so becomes a powerful way for you to frame your solution, proving to your customer that you have listened, that you have heard her, and that what she has said matters. Remembering and repeating customer words proves that you understand her situation, her needs, and her priorities. It goes a long way in building the kind of rapport that helps her see you as a trusted advisor.

So, for instance, if your customer tells you that she needs assurance from you that you can provide a flexible solution that will accelerate performance in the long term, be precise in how you answer her. Don't reframe the issue and tell her that you can offer a simple solution that will speed up performance. Use her phrasing to say, "I can assure you that, yes, we can provide a flexible solution that will accelerate performance in the long term."

Don't use synonyms. Don't find a fancier or simpler way of repeating her request. Remember her words. Repeat her words. And in doing so you will prove that communicating with her in her terms is important to you.

Summarize and Validate

Another way to show that you are actively listening is to summarize and validate the issues you have discussed. Doing so will confirm in your customer's mind that you have heard her and that you have understood her needs and priorities.

At key junctures, quickly summarize what you've heard and confirm. For example, you might say, "So, as I understand it, you're looking for fulfillment details about Product X with a focus on timing. Is that correct?" In that exchange, you've summarized and validated—two critical items that are crucial for moving on to next steps in the sales process.

Our research has shown that this is a step too many sales professionals skip. Often it's because they want to avoid making the impression that they haven't been listening or paying attention or that they don't understand. Sometimes they don't summarize and validate because they think it's a waste of time. But this isn't true. While you don't want to sound like a parrot as you repeat the customer's words and confirm what she's been saying, it is important to make it clear that the conversation has been a two-way street with understanding on both sides.

Summarizing and validating are key steps in the active listening process. Listening for content, meaning, and feeling; identifying vocal qualities and body language; and remembering customer words prepare you for the kind of active listening that will put you in good stead with your customer as you discover more about her needs. By listening to your customer, you can discover much about what she needs and what her priorities are. If you get this right, you can accelerate the sales process and close more deals.

Critical Moment: Deal with Early Price Requests

Sometimes it's not the sales professional who is rushing the sales process but the customer. In many cases, this takes the form of early price requests.

Oftentimes, early on in the sales process, your customer will start asking about price—well before you've had a chance to build value, investigate your customer's needs, or discover which solutions might be most appropriate.

This can be a particular challenge if you're not the low-price leader in your category. Companies that go out there with the lowest prices might lead with this benefit. But in most cases, companies aren't selling on price; they're selling on other values.

Generally, you don't want to disclose price before you've had a chance to discover your customer's needs and build value for him. Sometimes though, despite your best efforts, your customer insists on pushing the conversation toward price. In order to buy some time, there are a couple ways to handle early prices discussions while still assuring the customer that he will get the information he wants.

- **Tactfully Delay the Price Discussion.** Delaying the price discussion requires some finesse. You don't want to irritate the customer by appearing to be evasive or acting as though you didn't hear the question. The key here is to shift the conversation so that you can discover a bit more about the customer and his needs before discussing pricing. You might say, for example, "I'd be happy to provide pricing information. As you know, there are a number of options with this service. If I could ask you a few more questions so that I can better understand your needs, we can work up a specific quote from there."
- **Give a Price Range.** Sometimes the customer's number-one need really is to know the price—and he won't budge until he knows what that price is. Respect that. We suggest providing a range based on the information you have gathered so far during the discovering phase. You might say something along the lines of, "We take pride in offering solutions that work with every budget. On the low end of the scale, you're looking at $X, while at the high end, you'd be looking at $XY. Let's talk about where in that spectrum you and your organization might fit based on your needs."

If your customer is persistent on the pricing question, remember that your answer is always yes—"yes, and," meaning

(continued)

(*continued*)

that yes, you can address the pricing issue in broad strokes and you'd like to continue to discover more about the customer's needs and priorities by asking more questions so that you can provide accurate pricing based on his needs.

Avoid Common Pitfalls

Getting to know your customer's needs and priorities is a critical step in the sales process. Research has confirmed this fact in myriad studies—our own and others. Asking the right questions and actively listening to what your customer has to say can help you tailor solutions to meet her needs and accelerate the sales process, allowing you to close more deals. But sometimes this is easier said than done, and it's easy to make some missteps along the way. Because discovering is a critical step in the sales process, we want to highlight some of the common pitfalls and discuss ways to avoid them.

Don't Assume

One of the easiest traps sales professionals can fall into—especially for those who have been in sales for a while—is to assume they already know what the customer wants, what his needs are, what his priorities are, what he wants to discuss, and so on. We've already mentioned the dangers of making assumptions, but it bears repeating.

Oftentimes, sales professionals believe they know where a customer is headed with a particular line of conversation or that they know what a customer is thinking. But it's important to remember that every customer is unique and that every situation is as well. The worst thing you can do as a salesperson is assume. Once you start making assumptions, you close your mind to hearing important information. Even if a customer says what you thought he was going to say, it's still important to listen as you might very well glean important insight into his needs and priorities by hearing how he says what he says as well as what he doesn't say. It's important to keep an open mind and to keep listening, even if you think you're about to hear something you've heard countless times before from countless different customers.

Don't Get Too Far ahead of Your Customer

Asking the right questions and actively listening to your customer's responses while paying attention to her body language and remembering her key words and phrases while analyzing what she's saying and not saying and how she's saying it while thinking ahead about how to address her concerns—well, that's not always easy. There's a lot going on there, and it's easy to get distracted by trying to figure out what to say next.

Being fully engaged in a conversation with your customer while anticipating what will be said next is tricky. While your customer is giving you information, you're already analyzing and thinking about the meaning. The trick here is to slow down. Use your questioning skills and active listening skills to maintain focus on the customer and what she needs to discuss. Remember that if you listen to your customer, she'll tell you exactly what she needs.

Don't Interrupt the Customer

One thing we see among many sales professionals is a tendency to interrupt customers. It's a common thing to do when you think you already know what they are going to say next. As an example, in an effort to show a customer how knowledgeable you are, you might cut him off midsentence, saying, "Oh! I know exactly what you're talking about. You like Widget A because it's more efficient."

Jumping the gun this way is a mistake. Although you might just be trying to show that you're in tune with the customer or that you really know your product, interrupting doesn't give the customer a chance to say what he wants to say, nor does it give you a chance to listen to your customer and discover more about his needs. The more you interrupt the customer, the less likely he is to open up and keep providing you with the information you need.

Sometimes the customer simply wants to verbalize for himself what he and his organization needs. There's a certain psychology behind providing your customer with a solution that he himself just verbalized. Letting your customer be heard, repeating his words, and validating what you've heard are critical steps in the sales process. Don't rush the process by interrupting.

Don't Abandon Discovering

Just as it can be easy to rush the process, sales reps too often want to move too quickly from discovering to presenting. They want to show the customer that they know what she wants and that they have exactly the product for her. This is a mistake. It not only leaves the customer with the impression that the thing foremost in your mind is selling her a widget but also makes it difficult to build the kind of rapport that will lead to long-lasting relationships that improve sales over the long haul.

Asking the right questions and actively listening to the answers allows you to get a full picture of your customer's needs and priorities. Don't be afraid to dig deep here in order to gather quality information. Doing so not only proves that you are interested in your customer but also helps you hone your presentation so that you can tailor your solution to her precise needs. Rushing through the discovering process so that you can launch into your presentation too often leads to holes in your presentation or—worse yet—presenting the wrong solution altogether.

Top performers spend more time in the planning and discovering phases of the sales process than in presenting and closing. In fact, solid planning and thorough discovering builds momentum that naturally leads to a successful presentation and a profitable close.

The importance of the discovering phase of the sales process cannot be overemphasized. Discovering your customer's needs is a critical step in the sales process, because his needs are what drive buying opportunities. It is those needs that spark the motivation to purchase and provide the impetus to ultimately make a purchasing decision. Top-performing sales professionals understand that it is during this phase that they have a tremendous opportunity to continue to build rapport, understand their customer's needs and priorities, and discover the quality information that will allow them to tailor solutions that fit. Asking the right questions and actively listening to the answers are critical when it comes to discovering what your customer needs. Doing so also goes a long way in helping you become a trusted advisor—one whose insights into your customer make for a compelling presentation that accelerates the sales process and allows you to close more deals. We'll talk about presenting next, in Chapter 6.

Critical Selling: Lessons Learned

- Discovering information about your customer, her organization, and their needs is a critical step in the sales process and should never be rushed. Top performers typically consider this phase of the process to be the most important.
- Top-performing sales reps dig deep to discover the root cause of their customers' needs, asking targeted questions that go beyond the surface to focus on key areas in order to uncover high-quality information about needs and priorities.
- Modeling your questioning and listening skills after effective interviewers such as Larry King, Barbara Walters, and Oprah Winfrey can help you master the art of discovering to ask the right questions in the right way at the right time.
- Discovering should feel like a natural, positive conversation full of open- and closed-ended questions. Top-performing sales professionals focus their questions on customer situation, customer needs and challenges, the people and relationships that

drive decision-making, the customer's buying process, the options and alternatives the customer is considering, and the impact the purchase decision will have on the customer and his organization.

- Studies have shown that listening might well be the most important skill that salespeople can possess. Top performers understand that actively listening to customers means more than just hearing words. It also means paying attention to what customers say and do not say as well as how they say what they say.

- Top-performing sales reps listen for content, meaning, and feeling. They cue-in on tone, pace, and inflection. They pay attention to body language. They remember and repeat their customers' words and phrasing. And they summarize and validate what the customer has said. And they do this for every conversation with each customer.

- Asking the right questions and actively listening is usually more difficult than it seems, and it's easy to make some missteps. Top performers strive to avoid common pitfalls such as making assumptions about their customers, getting too far ahead of their customers, rushing the sales process, and abandoning the discovering phase too early in order to launch into presenting.

6

Presenting What Your Customer Needs: Link a Tailored Solution

YOU'VE CONNECTED WITH the customer and set the stage for a positive sales interaction by delivering a solid opening. You've done your research, looking into your customer and his organization. You've asked the right questions and listened to the answers. You're building credibility and trust and are on your way to becoming a trusted advisor.

So far, so good.

Now it's time to move forward and deliver your presentation to your customer, that winning presentation that you give to all your best customers, the presentation that you've rehearsed and delivered so many times that you have it down pat. You could do it blindfolded. You eat that presentation for breakfast.

Right?

Wrong.

If this is your approach to making presentations, you're missing a big opportunity. Presenting isn't about delivering a canned performance that simply highlights you, your organization, and your product or service. It's your opportunity to share with your customer a tailored solution that's linked to his needs, accommodates his priorities, and fulfills the objectives of his purchasing decision. It's not the time to regurgitate the same old presentation that you always give.

It's important to keep in mind that all customers are different. The reasons each customer will purchase your product or service are as varied as your customers themselves. Therefore, your biggest opportunity to deliver a presentation that will win the sale comes down to your ability to demonstrate how your product or service will meet that particular customer's unique needs.

Don't waste all the time and energy you've expended up to this point in getting to know your customer, asking questions, and actively listening to his answers by delivering the same presentation you always give.

Presenting is about sharing a tailored, customized solution with your customer and linking what you can offer to his specific needs and priorities. It's not something you should do by rote. Instead, a presentation that really hits the mark requires you to take advantage of what discovering revealed, plan the approach, tailor the solution, and ask for feedback.

Take Advantage of Discovering

Your presentation can be only as powerful as the information you gathered earlier in the sales process. The more detailed the information you have discovered about your customer, the more effective your presentation will be. In fact, thorough discovery not only helps you learn more about your customer but also, when done well, gives you the confidence you need to make an excellent presentation.

Asking the right questions and actively listening to the answers in the discovering phase of the selling cycle helps you guide your customer through his decision-making process, think deeply about the issues that are important to him, discuss his needs and priorities, and articulate what matters (and what doesn't). When you've helped your customer think carefully about his needs and priorities, you are better positioned to offer insights and ideas and to deliver a tailored, customized presentation that meets your customer's needs because you know that what you have to say will resonate with him.

There is power in simplicity when it comes to presenting. Top-performing sales professionals understand the importance of linking the features and benefits of their products or services to the specific needs and priorities of their customers. Presenting isn't about discussing every single piece of data, every specification, every feature, and every benefit. It's not about delivering a twenty-minute monologue accompanied by eighty PowerPoint slides. It's about sharing a targeted presentation that identifies solutions in a way that is tailored to meet the customer's needs. Doing so allows the customer to buy in to the value of your product or solution, the value of your organization, and the value of working with you rather than with your competition.

This is especially true for products that are technical in nature. For example, TriZetto, a division of Cognizant, provides world-class information technology solutions to make better health care happen. Their list of features is huge and complex, full of technical specifications. Their sales team fully understands their products, and it can be easy for them to get carried away touting all the features and benefits of their software solution. But they also know that if the customer doesn't care about it, it doesn't matter.

Translation: keep it targeted. The best sales presentation isn't one that goes on and on about numerous features. It's about sharing with your customer the information that is most important to him. Top-performing sales reps know how to customize the presentation and the level of detail in it to match the customer, his communication style, the time allotted, and, of course, the customer's needs and priorities. This means you have to think about each presentation you give to each customer. You have to plan your approach.

Plan the Approach

There are no shortcuts here. All too often, salespeople are looking for tricks, silver bullets, or new techniques, seeking some surefire way to shorten the sales cycle, to win the customer's business, and to move on to the next client. But the truth is that there are no shortcuts or tricks when it comes to being a top-performing sales rep.

There are no shortcuts when it comes to delivering effective sales presentations that are on the mark. Each customer should get a different presentation, because each customer's needs are unique. This customer is different from all your other customers—her organization is different, and her needs and priorities are different. Who you're talking to matters, as do her needs, priorities, and objectives. Don't drop the ball at this stage by trying to take a shortcut and giving her the same presentation you give every customer. Instead, plan a unique presentation for each unique customer.

Imagine what might happen if you choose not to plan for each sales presentation. What might be the risks or costs of failing to plan? Top performers understand that those risks are numerous:

- You might forget to mention important pieces of information.
- You might lose sight of the customer's highest-priority needs.
- You might drone on too much about information the customer doesn't care about.
- You might oversell your solution and create new issues and concerns in the customer's mind.
- You might not be able to clearly differentiate your solution from the competition or from alternatives your customer is considering.
- You might not be prepared to handle tough questions or objections from the customer.

The ways in which you could foul up a presentation are countless. We say that not to frighten or discourage you but to emphasize the importance of planning for each presentation.

When you think about how you want to tackle a presentation, think back to what you learned during the discovering phase. This is a critical step when it comes to making effective presentations. Take a look at what you found to be among the customer's six critical areas of focus. Highlight the words that she used again and again. Make a list of her needs and then prioritize them, ranking them from most important to least important. Consider, too, your customer's style: Is she friendly and personable? Business-oriented? A visionary? Cautious and skeptical?

Think about how you should fine-tune your approach in order to accommodate her style. Take the time to think through how your solution meets her needs and to consider the level of detail that will be required to deliver. It's also important to consider your competition and the alternatives she is considering. How does your solution line up? How will you differentiate? What key areas should you focus on? You also will need to consider who, from the customer's organization, will be attending your presentation. What are their individual needs? What do they care about most or want to avoid? Finally, you should think through the tough questions or objections you might face and what your responses might be.

Top-performing sales reps take all these factors into consideration, capitalizing on everything they've learned during the sales process, from the initial call through the discovering phase. You can see here how Critical Selling really is a framework: each phase builds on the last. The information, knowledge, and insight you have gleaned during each stage all come together now so you can make the most effective presentation possible, one that is uniquely tailored to your customer's needs and wins the sale.

There's no need to rush through this—it might take ten minutes; it might take a half hour. The amount of time will be determined by the complexity of the solution being offered. The critical point here is that you are synthesizing the information you've gathered so far so that you can really think about the best approach to give your customer what she needs. Everything you do while planning the approach will help you tailor a solution specifically for your customer.

Tailor the Solution

Now that you have taken the time to prepare and think through the key components about the customer and your offerings, the next step is to take that information and use it to craft an actual presentation. This is easier said than done, and in our experience, sales professionals need a framework to follow when putting their presentations together.

Unfortunately, we come across way too many organizations, and sales reps, that all too often fail to effectively present their solutions in ways that resonate with their customers. For example, we recently worked with a global consumer packaged-goods company, with more than 2,000 sales professionals, that was focused on contractual sales. This outmoded mentality prevented them from engaging in needs-focused dialogues with their customers. As a result, they faced challenges in gathering through discovering the kind of information that would lead to mutually beneficial outcomes. In addition, the company's sales reps were eager to jump straight to closing without presenting to their customers the details about how their products and services could meet their customers' needs. In essence, the company had to find a way to show their customers that not only were their sales reps focused on the needs of their customers but also the solutions they could provide would support the short- and long-term business objectives of their customers. They had to learn how to tailor each and every solution they proposed to each individual customer and the unique needs of those customers.

Top-performing sales professionals understand that it is critical to tailor every sales pitch to each customer's specific needs and wants. They also know how important it is to demonstrate some versatility in the process, modifying their approach for each customer. And they understand how tailoring the solution—and the presentation—helps them not only to win trust and drive the deal to completion but also to establish long-lasting professional relation-ships that result in more business.

We have identified a framework comprised of three critical steps to delivering a winning presentation:

1. Transition
2. Recommend
3. Connect

Following these three steps in this order helps sales reps deliver the most effective presentations. Let's look at the steps in order.

Transition

Your presentation might come toward the end of a single conversa-tion, or it might follow a series of discussions with your customer. Either way, it's important to signal to your customer that you're moving from the discovering phase, which has been a full-fledged conversation replete with questions and answers, to the presenting phase. The transition allows you do to that, signaling to your customer that you're shifting from identifying needs to sharing information. An easy and effective way to do this is to thank the customer for his time, ask if he wants to discuss anything else, and then let him know that you'd like to provide information to him that speaks to his needs and priorities.

Transitioning is as simple as saying something along the lines of, "Mr. Smith, thanks so much for taking the time to discuss your objectives and what is important to you. If you don't have any other questions at this point, I'd like to share a solution that I'm confident will meet your needs." The key here is to build a bridge between the discovering phase and the presenting phase, acknowledging what the customer has told you and signaling that, together, you are going to move to the next phase.

Your customer should be ready for this. By this point in the process, you should be on the same page, in sync with one another about next steps. If, however, your customer makes it clear that he's not ready to move to the presenting phase, then it's likely you've missed something along the way. Remember to listen to your customer and watch for flags that might indicate hesitation. If you've followed the steps up to this point, your customer should be ready for the presentation. But if he isn't, be flexible. Let him have the floor to address any lingering questions he might need to ask or to voice any objections he might have—and then address them and be ready to move on to presenting.

Recommend

After you've voiced that you're transitioning from discovering to presenting, it's time to recommend the solution that you are proposing to the customer. This should be a concise statement, delivered confidently—especially because, by this point, you should feel completely comfortable in recommending a solution to your customer.

It's critical at this juncture, when choosing the words you will use for your recommendation, to be specific. Cite the product or service or collection of products or services you are recommending. Remember that your recommendation is part of the value you provide as a trusted advisor. With that, it's important that the recommendation statement come first. After you've stated your concise, specific recommendation, you can go deeper into the features and benefits and how they link to your customer's needs. Your recommendation could be something simple and brief, such as, "Based on the discussions we've had, I am recommending the Gold Edition of Product X with the professional service plan, both for your technicians and for your field reps."

Remember to keep it simple here. Just a well-planned sentence or two should do the trick. After you've made this statement, then you can take the time to explain why you are making the recommendation and how the features and benefits of the recommendation will connect to your customer's needs.

Connect

Now is your chance to connect the dots. Here is where most of the presentation lives. You're connecting the dots, linking your customer's needs to the solution you have recommended and the features and benefits that come along with that solution. At this juncture, it's critical to state the needs that have been identified, highlight the features and benefits, and clearly explain how your solution meets the customer's needs.

Remember to address all of the customer's concerns and to present your solution in a way that matches your customer's list of priorities. Think back to the discussion above in "Plan Your Approach." This is why it's critical to rank your customer's six critical areas of focus and his list of needs and priorities. You want to connect your solution and its features and benefits on a one-to-one basis with your customer's needs and priorities.

When making this connection, you want to show the customer how the solution meets each of his needs. You want to explain the features, benefits, and potential outcomes for the customer. Remember to use the customer's words so that you can connect the dots in his vernacular. You might say, "I understand how important improving response time is for you so that your employees can more quickly access customer data. Several aspects of the Gold Edition will save time and allow for more efficient client interactions. Let's walk through them."

And then, here, right at this point, is when you get into the meat of your presentation. It's critical that you go about this in a well-planned manner, addressing each of the customer's needs that he shared with you. His first priority is X; here's how your product can give him X. He needed Y; this is how your product can address that need. He wanted Z; here's how this product can deliver Z. Tackle each and every need and priority. Connect the dots between each of his needs and your solution.

Tailoring the solution to your customer's needs, priorities, and objectives is critical when it comes to becoming the kind of trusted advisor who closes more deals. Remember to link the solution to his needs and to keep each point of the presentation targeted. Present the specific information that this particular customer needs and wants. And then listen to what he has to say.

Critical Moment: Avoid Common Pitfalls When Presenting

Presenting well requires some skill and finesse. The good news is that these skills are learnable; with practice they will become second nature. The bad news is that there are myriad ways for sales professionals to derail a presentation. By becoming aware of some common pitfalls, you can strive to avoid making mistakes that might cost you the sale.

- **Don't Deliver a Canned Presentation.** We cannot emphasize this enough. If all your presentations sound the same, it's a red flag. Each presentation needs to be tailored to each individual customer based on what you have learned during discovering. The features and benefits you mention and the level of detail you go into should vary for each customer. It is critical to tailor each presentation to the unique needs of every individual customer. It's a huge pitfall to do a good job in discovering customer needs and then deliver a canned presentation. This can frustrate a customer regarding the time he spent with you and can move you further away from reaching trusted advisor status.

- **Don't Be Inflexible.** Another common pitfall is to be too set in what you plan to discuss even if the topic is not relevant to the customer. All too often, sales reps put their own preferences before the needs of the customer. This is a mistake. The presentation is about the customer first, and if the customer throws you a curve ball, you have to have the ability to adapt and be flexible so that you can spend most of your time discussing what's important to him.

- **Don't Bury Your Customer in Information.** In the new sales environment, your customer can easily find information about you, your organization, and your product and services, whether through colleagues, on your website, through social media, or anywhere else on the Internet. There's no sense in repeating information that your customer can easily find and read elsewhere. Your customers want a salesperson who can offer a tailored recommendation linked to their needs. Your job is to provide expertise—not to be a walking brochure. Deliver a presentation that highlights the benefits that directly address your customer's key priorities.

- **Don't Forget to Focus on Your Customer.** Your presentation should feel less like a speech and more like a lively conversation between you and your customer. Don't forget to include her in your discussion. Be sure to allow time for your customer to ask questions throughout the presentation, and be sure you ask questions of her as well. In fact, it's important to be flexible and let your customer interject with questions at any point during the presentation. Don't make her wait until the end of your spiel to ask questions; this can cause you to lose the opportunity to hear what your customer has to say and to deliver information that better meets her needs. Let her have the floor. Keep the dialogue open. And be sure that the presentation is all about her.

- **Don't Push Your Own Agenda.** Of course you want your customer to buy what you're selling. That's a given. But it's important to make the purchase decision about fulfilling your customer's needs, not about selling another widget. Show your excitement about the customer achieving her desired outcome. It's easy to see the difference between a

(continued)

(*continued*)

sales professional who just wants to sell something and one who is genuinely interested in and excited about helping his customer.

- **Don't Be Afraid to Revisit the Land of Discovery.** In the interest of wrapping up the presentation and moving toward closing, it can be easy to not connect all the dots that link your customer's needs to the solution you have tailored just for her. Pay attention to the customer and for any signs that she might be hesitant, that she might not agree with what you've presented, or that she might not fully understand how your solution meets her needs. Don't be afraid to walk it back a bit and revisit the discovering process. You can always go back to the "Land of Discovery" and ask more questions in order to flush out what concerns your customer has. If needed, taking some time during presenting to revisit discovering can help you strengthen your solution (discussed below) and make your customer feel more comfortable about the purchase decision.
- **Don't Rush the Process.** During no point in the sales process should you push forward if the customer isn't ready. It's a common pitfall for sales reps to fall into that old always-be-closing mentality, but that almost always backfires. Don't rush your customer through the sales process. Allow her time to ask questions. Listen to her answers. Ask for feedback. Address alternative options that she is considering. Discuss what the consequences of her go or no-go decision might be.
- **Don't Avoid Dealing with Objections or Negative Feedback.** All too often, it can be easy for sales reps to take objections or negative feedback personally, becoming defensive in the wake of what they perceive to be a potentially insurmountable roadblock on the path to

closing the deal. But the truth is, if your customer has a concern, getting no feedback at all is worse than getting negative feedback. At least you have a chance to deal with the negative feedback. You can address objections. In fact, top-performing sales professionals consider objections as opportunities to discover more about their customers, strengthen the proposed solution, and build trust. Don't shy away from having the conversation that can open the door to dialogue that could help you further educate your customer about the benefits of your solution and how well the solution will meet her needs.

Ask for Feedback

After you've presented a tailored solution to your customer based on his needs, priorities, and objectives, don't think you can close your presentation with a clap of your hands and a quick "Let's get this contract signed!"

No, top-performing sales reps know that the end of their presentation isn't the end of the discussion. They understand that the next step after presenting a tailored solution is to ask for feedback. It's important to keep the lines of dialogue open so that you can make sure your customer understood what you just said, so that he can ask any questions, and so that you can ensure that he is satisfied with the solution you offered. With that, it's important to ask for feedback.

Oddly enough, this is one of those steps that too many sales-people either ignore or miss entirely. To some sales professionals, it's just not natural or obvious to ask for feedback. Too many sales reps don't understand the value of asking for feedback, and so they believe that after presenting, they should immediately move on. But that kind of thinking is flawed.

The more frequently you ask your customer to move forward when he isn't ready, the more likely you are to lose his trust. Pushing your customer toward closing is a surefire way to convince him that all you care about is the sale—when what you should be doing is getting feedback on your recommendation to ensure he sees it the same way you do. By doing so, you show the customer you care about his opinion, and this continues to move you closer to becoming a trusted advisor.

Asking for feedback is a critical step. A simple "How does that sound?" tells your customer that you're still in a two-way conversation. It tells your customer that you still want to hear what he has to say, and that his opinion matters.

In fact, your customer should always feel that the two of you are having a conversation, even during the presenting phase. Your presentation should feel as though, together, you're having an active discussion focused on his needs, priorities, and objectives. A compelling, effective presentation should be a two-way street, not a soliloquy about you, your organization, and your product or service. Don't get caught up in a long-winded monologue that bores your customer to tears.

Asking for feedback is a critical component of that conversation. If you don't ask for feedback, you run the risk of assuming that he agrees that your solution meets his needs. When you do ask for feedback, you open the door for your customer to provide you with an indication of what he's thinking:

- A positive reaction (e.g., nodding head, smile, overt verbal agreement) could signal that it is, in fact, the right time to move to closing.
- A neutral reaction (e.g., blank stare, silence) might mean that you need to further explore what the customer is thinking, how he feels about the solution you have proposed, and whether this might be a time to strengthen your solution by asking more questions.

■ A negative reaction (e.g., head shaking, closed body language, overt verbal disagreement) should initiate additional questioning and should serve as an opportunity to work through any objections.

Top performers are never afraid to ask for feedback. They see this critical step as an opportunity to gain further insight into their customer—and to prove to the customer that they are more than just order takers looking to close a deal. Asking sincere, open-ended questions designed to solicit the customer's opinion about the proposed solution provides the customer with yet another chance to voice any concerns he might have.

Asking for feedback can be done with a simple question such as, "Based on what I've told you about this solution, how does it sound to you?" or "Now that you've heard about how this solution addresses your key issues, how well do you think it will meet your needs?" or "After hearing all of this, does this sound like the right solution for you?"

Ask questions and listen to the answers. Give your customer the opportunity to talk. Encourage honest feedback. Allow him to speak openly. Don't pressure him to agree with you; rather, ask open-ended questions simply to gather more information. And remember that even negative feedback is an opportunity—it's another chance for your customer to view you as a trusted advisor, another chance to keep learning about your customer, and another chance to further explain how your solution fits his needs.

Strengthen the Solution

When delivering your presentation to your customer, her needs and your solutions must be at the core of your presentation. However, there are a few tactics you can leverage in order to strengthen the impact of your delivery and take your presentation to the next level.

These include utilizing social proof, addressing alternative options, and acknowledging consequences.

Utilize Social Proof

Social proof is that psychological phenomenon whereby people are influenced by the actions or decisions of other people. It's one of Dr. Robert Cialdini's "Six Principles of Influence" (sometimes called the "Six Weapons of Influence"), which identify various ways in which organizations garner support for their product or service. The concept of "buzz marketing" falls within this sphere, as does "word-of-mouth marketing." Popular websites such as Angie's List, TripAdvisor, and Yelp work as well as they do because they capitalize on the power of social proof.

In essence, social proof argues that what has worked for others will work for you as well. Utilizing social proof with your customers instills confidence in them because it proves to them that others with like needs have had success with the solution you're sharing with them. Social proof consists of anecdotal evidence, data, statistics, case studies, and real-world examples. Positive reviews and customer referrals also fall into this category.

Sharing social proof with your customer provides him with an additional level of comfort, not least of which because it shows him that there is safety in numbers, particularly when you can point to evidence that proves that customers of a similar nature are satisfied with your product or service. Social proof can make your customer feel more confident about his purchase decision, and it can be a great opportunity for you to layer in benefits.

For example, when utilizing social proof, you might say, "During the past six months, we have successfully supported 500 customers who opted for our Gold Edition of Product X with the professional service plan because they know it offers better coverage and lowers long-term cost of ownership," or "More than 85 percent of *Inc. 5000* companies have chosen the Gold Edition of Product X with the professional service plan to meet their business needs because they appreciate how much time it saves their technicians and field reps."

Pairing data with benefits is a powerful one–two punch that helps your customer feel more confident in going with the solution you have provided. Utilizing social proof allows you to gently but effectively guide your customer forward in the buying decision while strengthening your solution.

Address Alternative Options

In addition to utilizing social proof, another way to strengthen the solution is to address alternative options. If at some point you learn that your customer is considering—or even leaning toward—other options (i.e., your competitors), address the alternatives head on.

Don't shy away from this conversation. Don't pretend that yours is the only option, particularly if your customer has made it clear that he's considering alternatives. It's best to get the issue out in the open. Top-performing sales professionals see this as an opportunity to show the customer that they are willing to explore all of the options they are considering. Furthermore, they find productive ways to discuss alternatives with their customers to help them make the best decision.

It's critical to keep in mind that doing what's best for the customer is the best thing you can do as a sales professional. Do right by your customer. Acknowledge the fact that he's considering other options and discuss them with him. Do so in a positive way. Help the customer see how the solutions compare to one another and then highlight the areas where you can better meet the customer's needs, especially those that are at the top of his priority list.

So, for example, in addressing alternatives you might say something along the lines of, "It sounds as though you're looking at the Bronze Edition of Product Y offered by Company OtherGuy. They certainly do offer some strong features in that area, which help companies meet their customers' expectations. You shared earlier that what's most important to you is purchasing a quality product while lowering the overall cost of ownership. Our product focuses more in these areas and is proven to drive down the long-term ownership costs without sacrificing quality."

Directly addressing alternative options helps you earn trust in the eyes of your customers. When your customers see that you're willing to bring out in the open an issue that could potentially derail your sale, they think, "I can trust this guy." This is very powerful.

You're always better off in the long term when you address the various options your customer is considering. Your customer is already thinking about it anyway, so it's best to address the issue head on. Ask what your customer likes about the other options. Ask how your solution compares. And then use that feedback to layer in features and benefits for your product or service, showing your customer where the value lies in going with you and your organization. Even if you end up losing the sale, remember that you've established in your customer's mind that you're more than just a sales rep looking to close a deal; you're a trusted advisor to whom the customer can turn again and again in the future for advice and consultation. Just because it's a no now, it doesn't mean that it's a no forever.

Acknowledge Consequences

Utilizing social proof and addressing alternative options are effective ways to strengthen your solution. Another way to do just that is to discuss with customers what would happen if their needs go unsatisfied. Top-performing sales professionals know how powerful it can be to talk with their customers about the consequences of action and inaction. They find ways to discuss with their customers the potential impact of rejecting the proposed solution.

Just as any undertaking comes with risks, there also are risks associated with not doing something. As a sales professional, it's easy to think about the benefits of taking a certain action. Part of your job is to show your customer the risks he takes in delaying a decision or rejecting the proposed solution. This can be a little tricky.

Discussing consequences requires a little finesse. It's not pushing. It's not being argumentative. It's not frightening your customer with a list of negative effects. You can't be defensive when showing your customer what consequences he might face if he rejects your solution or puts it off. Instead, getting your customer to acknowledge consequences is about getting him to look at the other side of things and consider the risks of inaction. It's about being a consultant, someone who can provide valuable insights the customer might not be considering.

When tackling consequences, you might say, "It's important to consider these risks as you're finalizing your decision. Is there any concern about what might happen during, say, the next six months if you don't do this now? How will this affect your business?" or "It sounds as though you've been exploring options for several months. While it's great to know what else is out there, how concerned are you that your company might miss out on potential cost savings that you could start seeing now with the implementation of this solution?"

Asking questions that prompt your customer to consider the consequences of inaction or of opting for a competitor's product or service can be particularly effective when dealing with a customer who is hedging or seems reluctant to make any decision at all. But it's important to consider how you deliver this message. You don't want to come off as a pushy salesperson whose sole focus is on closing the deal. Getting your customer to acknowledge consequences has to be done in a way that allows you to demonstrate genuine concern and show that you have the customer's best interests in mind. In doing so, you can reiterate how your solution links to the customer's needs and addresses his priorities, talking about the key features and benefits that will have the most impact on your customer and his organization.

Critical Moment: Present Persuasively

Just as we have advised that you pay attention to your customer's body language, the words she uses, and her communication style, so too should you think about your own approach to communicating and presenting. What you say and how you say it can either increase the likelihood that your customer will accept your solution or decrease it. Becoming a skilled presenter takes some practice. Focusing on these four tips can help you present more persuasively:

- **Link Your Solution to the Customer's Values.** Really think about what the customer values most and link your features and benefits to those values. What your customer values most is what is going to inspire her to take action. Although a solution geared to features and benefits is a critical component in your presentation, remember that your customer is motivated by her values. What a customer values and what motivates a customer are uniquely personal to each individual. Think about what issues, words, terms, and phrases your customer has emphasized time and again and be sure to connect your solution to those concerns.
- **Make the Most of Vocal Qualities.** Voice inflection, emphasis, tone, pace, volume—all of that conveys a message to your customer. Make sure that how you're saying something is consistent with what you intend to say. Use a warm vocal tone, and put some energy behind your words (remembering to adjust your communication style to your customer's). Convey to your customer the passion and enthusiasm you feel for your product or service and for your organization. Let your confidence come through your voice.
- **Use Pauses Effectively.** Strategic pauses provide your customer the space and time she needs to think about

what you're telling her. Use pauses to let the information you've shared with your customer sink in. If there is something you want to stress, a strategically placed pause can help the customer soak it in. Most sales professionals tend to chatter on. In fact, we have found that the average salesperson waits only a second or two before repeating a statement or asking a question again when not getting a response from a customer. Remember that you need not fill every moment with words. Don't try to fill up the empty spaces in a conversation. Instead, use pauses to let your customer absorb what you've said.

- **Use the Customer's Words.** As we mentioned in Chapter 5, repeating to the customer the same words she has used when conversing with you can be a powerful tool. There are certain words a customer will use over and over again. When you present your solution to your customer, use those words. Using words that are familiar to the customer creates a certain level of comfort. When you use the customer's words, you are building trust because she knows that you have heard her. Remember here not to use synonyms, which simply force the customer to process the information you're sharing in a new and unfamiliar way. Certain synonyms, while similar, mean slightly different things, and that slight difference might not be what your customer is looking for. Also, people interpret words differently. It can be risky to use a synonym, and there's no value is doing a word exchange.

Presenting well requires a lot of finesse and a lot of layers. The key is to focus the presentation on your customer, linking your solution to what she values most, using vocal qualities to

(continued)

(*continued*)

convey confidence and enthusiasm, using strategically placed pauses, and repeating the customer's words in your presentation. Doing so will help you make the most of the time you have with your customer.

Link Your Solution

When it comes to making effective presentations, remember that linking is powerful. During a presentation, your objective should never be to ply your customer with as much information as possible, burying him in social proof and inundating him with endless lists of features and benefits. The information you present should be selected carefully and, most important, specifically linked to your customer's needs.

Linking is key. Identify your customer's needs, priorities, and objectives and focus your presentation on highlighting those critical issues—and only those critical issues. There is no need to include in your presentation every feature and benefit about your product or service, particularly those that aren't relevant to the customer. In fact, offering too many benefits can actually backfire, prompting the customer to wonder whether he's paying too much for a product or service that includes a bunch of features he doesn't need and doesn't care about. Overkill creates doubt, which does no good in helping your customer view you as a trusted advisor or in closing the deal.

Keep your presentation focused, targeted, and tailored. Your objective is to have a lively, engaging conversation with your customer that revolves around what he wants to accomplish. A compelling presentation is a two-way street that shares with the customer a detailed, customized solution that fits his needs.

Remember, too, that every moment and every comment count. Don't get carried away and engage in a long-winded presentation that bores your customer and does little to spark his interest in moving forward with you. Hit the nail on the head with a tailored approach and prove your worth to your prospect.

The most powerful presentation is focused on the customer, linked to his most pressing concerns, and uniquely tailored to his needs. It's the one that leaves the customer walking away thinking, "This is the perfect solution for our needs." An effective presentation should provide natural, positive momentum that gently guides the customer toward the buying decision. When done well, presenting serves as an effective bridge between discovering and closing. We'll discuss closing next, in Chapter 7.

Critical Selling: Lessons Learned

- Top-performing sales professionals never deliver canned presentations. Instead, they understand that an effective presentation is one that takes advantage of what discovering revealed, is one in which the approach is planned, and is one in which the solution is carefully tailored to meet the customer's needs.
- Top performers understand that winging a presentation offers far more risks than delivering a carefully planned, unique presentation to each customer. The risks of not planning vastly outweigh any costs associated with planning (e.g., time, energy, resources) and could lead to misunderstandings and unintended consequences.
- Delivering a presentation with a carefully tailored solution requires sales reps to follow a framework that focuses on three critical steps: transition, recommend, connect.
- Asking for feedback is a critical facet of every presentation. It's important to remember to include the customer in the presentation by asking him at various points during the conversation what he thinks about the solution you have offered him. Allowing your customer the chance to be heard during the presentation goes a long way in building trust.
- Utilizing social proof, addressing alternative options, and acknowledging consequences are effective ways to strengthen

the solution you have suggested to your customer. Doing so helps instill in him greater confidence in the purchase decision—and in you as a trusted advisor.

- Top performers understand how important it is to link their solution to the specific needs of the customer. Presentations that respect the customer's time, provide focused information targeted to the customer's needs and priorities, and allow the customer the opportunity to provide feedback should leave the customer thinking, "This is just what I need!"

7

Leverage Momentum at Closing: Capture Customer Confidence

CLOSING SHOULD BE a natural part of the sales process. It should capitalize on the momentum that you have established along the way. It's not a scheming tool or a tacky tactic or a cheesy gimmick. Nor is it a chance to manipulate your customer or to trick her into agreeing with you. Oddly enough, however, we have found that too many sales reps still lean on timeworn closing techniques that no longer work in today's selling environment. These sales reps still consider the Ben Franklin Close (also referred to as the Balance Sheet Close), the Option Close, and the Sympathy Close to be viable approaches.

This is a mistake.

Compiling a list of the negatives and positives in a pro-con format in no way brings you any closer to closing the deal or earning trusted-advisor status. Urging your customer to sign on the dotted line because you need to make quota or because this particular sale will win you a fabulous bonus or because you need to feed your family isn't going to help you build a lasting relationship that results in more sales down the road.

Unfortunately, closing techniques such as this remain more popular than anyone should care to admit. Maybe you've fallen back on techniques such as this in the past. It wouldn't be surprising: for years, sales managers and trainers taught these techniques, presenting them to sales reps as winning methods designed to secure deals. These couldn't be any more off target today.

Whether the Ben Franklin, the Option, or the Sympathy—or the Apology, the Cradle-to-Grave, the Puppy Dog, the Take-Away, or whatever (the list of tactics goes on and on)—the truth is that those approaches are just gimmicks. And when it comes to closing, gimmicks won't do the trick. This isn't *Glengarry Glen Ross*.

In today's world, closing simply comes down to two things: when to close and how to do it most effectively. As such, it requires a balanced mix of science and art: being confident without being cocky, persuasive without being pushy. Our research shows that when it comes to closing, top performers are those who can maintain that balance, harnessing the natural momentum of the sales process by fully following the Critical Selling framework and recognizing buying signals. They know how to help the customer move forward from being interested in the solution presented to making a commitment to it.

You should know when the time is right to close the deal: you've identified the customer's needs, presented a solution, and asked for feedback. Now it's time to move forward. We've identified four critical steps to secure a close:

- Summarize
- Gain commitment
- Define next steps
- Confirm

In essence, this is the time when you want to leverage the momentum of the sales call by confidently asking the customer to make a commitment, knowing he's motivated to agree to the solution you presented. You also want to make the closing actionable so your customer knows exactly what will happen next in the process. These four powerful steps will not only facilitate the closing but also allow your customer to continue to see you as a trusted advisor.

Summarize Where You've Been

You've presented your customer a tailored solution and asked for feedback, and you've addressed any lingering concerns. Your customer has indicated that he doesn't have any additional questions and that he's on board with the solution you offered. At this point, it's important to launch into the close—not necessarily with a bang but with a shift that signals to your customer that you're moving forward. Now is the time to recap what you and your customer have covered during the course of the sales conversation.

This is the point at which it's important to recap the key issues you've discussed with your customer and quickly go over the progress you've made during your time together. It's when you want to emphasize the customer's highest-priority needs and reiterate how your solution meets those needs. Doing so not only helps remind your customer of the sales journey you've been on together but also serves to instill further confidence in him, reminding him of how you've listened to his needs and tailored a unique solution linked to those needs. Summarizing where you've been helps your customer recall the collaboration you have enjoyed while conducting the due diligence necessary to arrive at this point.

When summarizing, you might say something along the lines of, "Nick, as you know, we've spent the past three weeks exploring how your company wants to improve logistics in its supply chain. We've been discussing the key areas in which strategic improvements can be made here, and we demonstrated how Product X can immediately improve efficiency by 25 percent or better."

You can be specific when summarizing, or you can speak in more general terms. The key is to make sure that you're on the same page as your customer. Doing so helps leave no doubt in your customer's mind that the right next step is to move forward. It also helps reduce any feeling of buyer's remorse your customer might have, since he is confident that you have had his back as a trusted advisor in what's been a constructive, collaborative selling conversation.

As natural as it might seem to summarize, it's actually not at all uncommon for sales reps to skip this step. Oftentimes, reps feel as though they've already covered this ground, particularly if they've asked for feedback during the presenting phase of the sales process. When you fail to summarize, however, you don't provide your customer with the last bit of confidence needed to move forward. You don't provide that additional opportunity for him to consider all of the work, time, and effort that was invested to get to this point. Nor do you offer the chance for him to come to the conclusion that it's the right time to move forward.

Summarizing provides one more juncture at which your customer can feel completely confident in the solution you have suggested. It gives him time to solidify his decision to sign with you. It's especially important to do so during complex sales with long selling cycles or with sales calls that have involved a lot of people. The extent to which you summarize (meaning, how in-depth you go with your recap) depends on how complex the sales call has been. But whether simple or complex, summarizing is a critical step in the closing.

Critical Moment: Find the Goldilocks Moment

When it comes to closing, timing is everything. Recognizing when to close is critical and, as with much throughout the selling cycle, it's a balance of art and science. Experienced sales professionals often gauge the best moment by intuition coupled with signals from the customer. But top performers understand that knowing when to close is very much about the process: if you've identified needs, presented a solution that meets those needs, and confirmed with the customer, it's time to proceed. If you've followed the process, the close should feel natural. If you're unsure, though, the time likely isn't right.

There are risks with getting the timing wrong. Closing too early can be just as bad (or worse) than closing too late.

- **Don't "Always Be Closing."** As we've said before, this tired old adage is as fallacious as it is outdated. One of the easiest ways to lose credibility and destroy any trust you've built with your customer is to close too early. The risks here are many. When rushing to close, your customer is likely to see you as nothing more than a salesperson desperate to sign a contract. It leaves the impression that all you care about is making the sale. It can easily make the customer feel that your goals matter more than his needs and priorities. If you're always closing, it's difficult (if not impossible) to try to go back and convince the customer that—oh, wait!—his needs do matter and that you want to discover more about them. Closing too early makes it much more difficult to win your customer's trust—and his business.

- **Don't Oversell.** Just as it can be fatal to always be closing, so can it be detrimental to never go for the close. Some sales reps just keep on talking, pumping up the benefits of their solution, listing each and every feature, going over every technical specification. Some reps keep asking questions, often to the point of needling the customer, usually out of fear that they haven't covered all their bases. Still others keep waiting for the customer to overtly indicate that he's ready to close the deal. You have to trust the process. If you've delivered a solid opening; researched your customer and discovered his needs, priorities, and objectives; and presented a tailored solution, it's probably time to move on to the next steps. If you've asked for feedback and confirmed with your customer, you've very likely come to the point when you have to ask your customer whether he's ready

(continued)

(continued)

to move forward. Don't miss your window of opportunity. Demonstrate confidence in the process—and in yourself— and guide your customer toward closing.

■ **Don't Fail to Trust the Process.** In between closing too early and closing too late is that Goldilocks moment—just the right time to close. If you've followed the process, the time is right. Once you've taken a complete inventory of your customer's needs and ensured that your customer understands the value of the solution you've presented, and once your customer confirms that your solution meets his needs, now is the time. He might also be demonstrating positive buying signs, or he might even give you clues here and there that could indicate his desire to move forward, but the key is to make sure that needs and solutions are fully aligned. Once you've gone through the process and gotten to that point, closing should be the natural next step.

Gain Commitment to Move Forward

Up to this point, from opening to discovering to presenting, you've consulted with your customer. You've recommended a solution. Now it's time to advocate for the solution you presented. As a trusted advisor, you've built the rapport and earned the credibility that allows you to ask for your customer's business. This is the moment of truth.

Gaining commitment from your customer to move forward is done in two important steps: advocate and then ask.

Advocate for Your Solution

This is the point when it's time to confidently let your customer know that the unique solution you have presented to him meets his needs. You want to reiterate that it's the right solution and that you fully support it.

When advocating for the solution you've presented, frame the conversation as one in which both you and the customer are participants. Use more "we" than "I" or "you." Emphasize that you and the customer are working together, that you're collaborating. Make sure that your customer sees what's in it for him and his organization. You might say something such as, "We've talked about how Product X will immediately begin to improve efficiency rates in your supply chain. Moving forward with this solution will be a giant step in the right direction for improving logistics for you and your organization. I'm confident we've found just the right solution for you."

Because you have done the right things in the sales process along the way and truly understand the customer's needs, you have earned the right to advocate for a solution. This statement is even more powerful if you are truly viewed as a trusted advisor. Customers who consider you a trusted advisor want your advice and your opinion. They want to know that an expert in this particular industry has carefully explored their needs and made a sound recommendation. This lends customers additional confidence in order to move forward.

Ask to Move Forward

It's never a good time to make assumptions, and now is definitely not the time to assume that your customer is ready to move forward. So, it's critical that you ask the customer to do so, directly and confidently.

Earlier, we discussed the importance of asking open-ended questions in order to discover information about your customer, his needs, and his priorities. Now, however, is the time for a closed-ended, yes-or-no question specifically designed to come to a decision. That question is not "Do you have any other questions?" which opens the door for more feedback rather than coming to a decision. Instead, the question should be something similar to, "Would you like to move forward with this solution today?" or "Are you ready to secure the order at this time?"

The key here is to ask the question, not to state what will happen next. Asking the question allows your customer the opportunity to confirm his agreement on moving forward.

Define Next Steps

As you continue to move forward with closing, building on the momentum, it's important to define the next steps, outlining for your customer what you will do together to finalize the deal, whether sending contracts, opening a purchase order, or issuing a memo of understanding.

It's important at this juncture to be clear and concise about what each of the next steps in the process are and what those steps entail. Be specific when discussing any technical aspects needed to get the deal done. It's critical that your customer understand not only what the next steps are, but also how they look. Make sure your customer knows who is doing what when. Delineate responsibilities and any deadlines so this important part of the sales process doesn't stall as a result of confusion, which could frustrate your customer and damage the close.

So, for instance, you might simply say, "For this next step, I will issue the paperwork to you as a PDF via e-mail. Please review it carefully, sign a copy, and return it to me by the end of the week via e-mail. I'll confirm receipt and have the document countersigned so we are ready to go first thing Monday morning."

Defining the next steps is one of those things that a lot of sales reps skip. It's easy to assume that your customer knows the drill or understands the process, even if you haven't worked together before. But leaving this to chance can cause confusion on the part of your customer, who might not know who is doing what next or what is expected of him. It might delay the sale, and it might frustrate your customer. None of that does any good—for your customer or you or your organization—and it certainly doesn't help you close the deal any faster. So, as a consultant who has your customer's best interests in mind, take the time to define for him exactly what the next steps in the process are so he isn't left wondering what will happen.

Critical Moment: Read the Signs—Carefully

Somewhere on the road between "always be closing" and "never be closing" are signs that point the way toward closing naturally. A natural close is one that leverages the momentum built during the entire sales process, from opening to discovering to presenting.

While you're traveling the path from opening to closing, it can be easy to get caught up in what might be considered signs that your customer is ready to jump to closing. She might say any number of things that could lead you to think that she's ready to sign on the dotted line:

"This sounds great!"

"I like what I'm hearing."

"All of this sounds just right."

"This all makes perfect sense."

Pay close attention here. Don't assume that any of these comments necessarily translate to "I'm in! Where do I sign?" because chances are your customer is simply agreeing to what you have said so far or merely indicating that you should proceed with whatever you plan to tackle next in the sales conversation. Buying signs should be considered more like directional signs. These signs indicate that things are going well, that the customer likes what she is hearing so far, and that you're on the right track. They do not mean it's time to pass go, collect $200, and sign the contract.

Don't rush the close, no matter how encouraging the signs might be. Don't let what you see as buying signs dazzle you into assuming that it's time to close. So, unless your customer overtly asks to close the deal by saying, "This is exactly what I need. Let's get the contract signed right now," keep the conversation going, follow the process, and close when the momentum naturally gets you there.

Confirm with Your Customer

Throughout the process, we've noted the importance of asking for feedback, of not making assumptions, of confirming. Doing so is no less important now. Although it can be easy to want to rush the process, confirming that your customer understands what happens next is a critical step.

We sometimes see sales reps who skip this step, usually because they don't want to risk an objection at this late stage in the game. But top-performing sales professionals understand that confirming is just about getting the customer to agree to the next steps that have been defined—not to the close itself. You've already taken care of that by advocating and asking.

With that, it's important to make sure that your customer fully understands what will happen next and who is responsible for what. Confirm responsibilities, tasks, and deadlines. This can be done with a simple question such as, "How do these next steps work for you?" or "Do those next steps all make sense?" or even just a quick "How does that sound to you?"

Closing isn't about pushing a contract in front of your customer. It's a conversation in which you've built rapport, collaborated with your customer, and earned the right to be considered a trusted advisor. It's about creating value, at every step throughout the sales process. That allows you to build on the positive momentum that moves you seamlessly from a solid opening all the way through to a confident close. Because closing should be the natural culmination of everything you've discussed so far with your customer, and he should feel confident that, together, you've devised a tailored solution that meets his unique needs.

Closing should be the natural next step in the sales conversation that you've been having with your customer. By the time you get to this point in the process, you've already done about 95 percent of the work, so closing should simply leverage the momentum you've already got going.

It's important to remember that the conversation you've been having with your customer, whether during one meeting or several, isn't just about getting to this point so you can close the deal. Building rapport, establishing credibility, and connecting with your customer aren't only about getting a signature on the dotted line. These things are about becoming a trusted advisor, a consultant who collaborates with her customer to do the best thing for him and his organization—whether you close this deal or the next one. Top-performing sales professionals understand the importance of following the process and reading buying signs, balancing the science and art of selling in order to secure the close with their customers.

Of course, closing doesn't always go the way we would like it to. From time to time, customers will have objections. Whether they come up at closing or even earlier in the process, if you're in sales, some objections are inevitable. We'll look at how to deal with objections next, in Chapter 8.

Critical Selling: Lessons Learned

- Top-performing sales professionals balance the art and science of closing well, harnessing the natural momentum of the entire sales call—from opening to discovering to presenting—in order to move the customer forward from being interested in the solution presented to making a commitment to it.
- Timing plays a big factor when it comes to closing. Top-performing sales professionals can identify the right time to close and know how to ensure that they don't close too early or too late and miss the opportunity.
- Summarizing what you have covered in the sales process thus far instills confidence in the customer that your solution meets his needs. It reminds him of the diligence you have done together and confirms that now is the right time to move forward. At closing is when it's time to shift from suggesting a solution to

advocating for it. As a trusted advisor, you have earned the right to reiterate to your customer your firm belief in the fact that the tailored solution you have suggested will meet his needs. It's time to gain commitment by advocating for your solution and asking your customer for his business.

- It's critical to define the next steps in the process so that your customer understands who is doing what when and what will happen next. After you've defined those steps, confirm with your customer that he fully understands them.
- A good close should allow your customer to feel confident that, together, you have come up with the perfect solution for his needs, and he should willingly agree to move forward to seal the deal.

8

Dealing with Objections:
Return to the Land of Discovery

OBJECTIONS: WHEN IT comes to sales, it's one of the issues sales professionals are most interested in. That's because all sales professionals, regardless of tenure or industry, have come face to face at least once with an insurmountable objection that they just couldn't overcome and, because of that, lost the sale.

These losses can for a long time nag sales professionals, who mull them over again and again, thinking that if they just could have overcome that one objection, they would have made the sale. These lost sales become the stuff of legends, those war stories about duking it out with customers—they hit you with an objection; you hit back with a solution. They hit you; you hit back.

All too often, objections result in epic battles between the customer and the sales rep—battles that, in all reality, no one actually wins. But objections should never turn into a battle of wills. Objections aren't about the battle, the art of war, or the sword and armor you bring to the table. Dealing with objections, rather, is about letting go and getting on the same side as your customer. Sales reps who try to overcome objections by showering the customer with more and more information, punch after punch, will struggle to close the deal—not to mention to build trust. But top-performing sales professionals understand that dealing with objections isn't about wearing down the customer. Top performers don't show up with a fighting mentality. Instead, they first seek to understand why the customer is objecting and then they take the time to learn about the customer's point of view in order to work toward a solution.

We understand that dealing with objections is a key issue for sales professionals. It's one of the trickiest challenges sales reps face and one of the main reasons why sales derail. But it doesn't have to be. In this chapter, we'll look at what objections are, why objections arise, how sales professionals can prepare for objections, how to reduce the number of objections, and, importantly, how to overcome any objection a customer can throw your way.

Recognize Real Objections

Defining what an objection is can be challenging—although we understand that you likely can recognize an objection when you hear one. The problem, though, is that some sales reps hear objections even where there aren't any. Instead, they hear objections in simple questions that customers ask just to better understand you and your product or service.

So let's look first at what objections are not. Objections are not questions about your company, products, or services; your approach; your previous track record; or how you compare to the competition. Objections should not be heard in questions such as these:

- How do I know your product will deliver on my expectations?
- What other solutions similar to this have you implemented?
- How does your product compare to that of Company OtherGuy?
- What service level guarantees do you offer?

Objections go beyond questions such as these. They are more than just challenging customer questions. Objections, rather, are statements that have the potential of stalling or ending the sales process altogether if not handled correctly. Real objections sound like this:

- I don't think you're the right fit for what we're looking for.
- The level of service you have outlined will not be sufficient for us.
- I'm not sure you can really deliver on the promises you're making.
- I don't think it's the right time to move forward with the solution you've presented.

Although most sales reps fear objections, the truth is that objections aren't such a bad thing. When a customer offers an objection, you have a critical opportunity to gain insight into his thought process and what he is concerned about—if you handle the moment the right way. You need to be able to uncover information about what is important to him and reveal the details about where your proposed solution has not met his expectations. Objections also can indicate areas that you didn't address properly or areas that you failed to cover adequately when discovering your customer's needs, values, and priorities. In fact, most objections arise not out of thin air but because something was missed during the sales process.

Understand Why Objections Come Up

Objections might be aired by a customer in any number of ways, but they usually boil down to one thing: the customer doesn't see the value in the solution you have presented. He doesn't see how a particular offering, product, or service meets his needs, either in whole or in part.

The reasons for this are varied, but, more often than not, it comes down to the fact that the sales professional didn't deliver.

We hate to say it, but it's true. Unfortunately, objections generally come up because the salesperson didn't get something right. There are any number of reasons why this might happen, including:

- The sales rep failed to connect with the customer and build rapport.
- The salesperson presented features and benefits before fully understanding the customer's needs.
- The salesperson presented a solution that was off the mark.
- The customer didn't feel that he was being heard by the salesperson.
- The salesperson tried to rush the sales process.

While we'll get into how to handle objections in just a moment, we want to share a thought: by reading this book, you have already begun dealing with objections, perhaps without even realizing it. By implementing the skills we've covered in this book, you will reduce the number of objections you receive from customers. It starts in the opening. Setting clear expectations and connecting with customers early on encourages them to open up and share information freely. This sets you up for your success during discovering as you ask the right questions and actively listen to the answers in order to truly understand your customers' needs. Once you have a complete understanding of their needs, you are well positioned to present compelling solutions that are linked to those needs. This provides you with the momentum you need to confidently advocate for your solution and gain agreement from the customer to move forward. In doing so, you have likely addressed objections that would have otherwise come up, which in turn accelerates the sales process and helps you close more deals.

Of course, that doesn't mean that you won't face any objections. In fact, it would be odd if you didn't hear at least one or two from your customer. The key is that you anticipate objections and handle them well.

Be Prepared for Objections

One of the most important aspects to handling objections effectively is being prepared for them. Planning plays a key role here. Think back to our discussion in Chapter 3, where we looked at why planning matters. Look back, too, to the precall planner we shared (see Figure 3.2). Planning is critical when it comes to anticipating not only your customer's needs, priorities, and values but also any objections he might have. It's a lot easier to handle objections when you're ready for them and have thought through how you might handle them.

Top performers understand this, and they learn to put themselves in their customers' shoes in order to prepare for objections that might arise during the sales process. This is good practice, and one that all sales reps, regardless of tenure or industry, can—and should—work on.

Think about your customer. In light of the needs, priorities, and objectives she has shared with you, ask yourself what objections might be lingering in the back of her mind. Is price going to be an issue? How might customer service issues affect the sale? What kind of timing, scheduling, or deadlines might give your customer pause? Are there any delivery, shipping, or logistics issues that might present a problem for her? Think about similar customers you have dealt with and recall the objections they have raised. How did you handle those concerns with those customers?

When you take the time to put yourself in your customer's shoes, you are better positioned to anticipate and handle any objections that she might raise.

Objections can pop up at any point in the selling cycle. Regardless of whether they arise during closing or at some other point in the process, the key issue isn't just when you handle them but also how you do so. In fact, how you handle those objections says a lot about you as a sales professional. It can be easy to become overwhelmed when faced with a barrage of objections. A lot of sales reps become defensive in the face of objections. But it's important to remain calm, polite, and professional when dealing with objections, and preparing will help you do so.

Remember, too, that top-performing sales professionals treat objections as opportunities. They not only prepare for objections but also handle them right away, directly and politely, instead of shying away from them or skirting the issue. Top performers also consider objections to be a good sign—a sign that their customers trust them enough to share their concerns with them. In fact, it's better that your customer open up to you about her objections than keep mum. When a customer voices her concerns, you have the chance to address them. If she keeps silent, you'll never know what you could have done better or differently.

We've done a lot of research into this area of the sales process, and we've discovered a few key things that top-performing sales reps do consistently to handle objections. In addition to putting themselves in their customer's shoes so they can anticipate objections that might arise, top performers follow a process to handle objections in a way that doesn't increase defensiveness and allows them to work through the concern side by side with the customer. They employ four critical skills that get to the heart of each objection so they can better address their customer's concerns (empathize, understand, address, and confirm).

Critical Moment: Take the Sting out of Objections and Rejections

When it comes to sales, objections and rejections simply come with the territory. Regardless of what service or product you sell, what industry you work in, and what kind of customers you deal with, objections and rejections are part of the game. Sales professionals hear "no" and "not now" and "maybe later" and even "never" more often than they would like. That's just the way it is.

It's easy to become discouraged by rejection or to become defensive in the face of objections. No one likes to get negative feedback, especially after spending a lot of time with a prospect. Fortunately, if you've followed the Critical Selling framework, connected with your customer, built rapport, and earned his trust, chances are strong that you'll face far fewer objections. But that doesn't mean you won't ever face any objections.

Top-performing sales professionals know that dealing with objections and handling rejection is very much about adopting a positive mindset. In fact, top performers welcome objections because they understand that it means their customers are comfortable enough with them to share negative feedback, which can be awkward and uncomfortable even for the toughest negotiators.

A positive attitude is critical when dealing with objections, and it might very well determine the outcome of your efforts. Consider every objection an opportunity to learn more about your customer. Think of an objection as valuable feedback that provides priceless insight into your customer's needs, priorities, and values. Don't look at an objection as a stopping block or a personal attack. Instead, use each and every objection as the means by which to discover what it is that is driving your customer's concern.

It can be difficult, but it's critical to not take objections personally. Take a step back. Slow down. Count to 10 if you have to. And then consider the issue from your customer's perspective. Ask him what it is about the issue that most concerns him and, most important, be open to listening to what your customer is saying and not saying.

Objections provide valuable information about what's important to your customer. They also lend considerable insight to where your product or service might not be on par with the competition. And, they might even tell you that you haven't spent enough time discovering your customer's key needs, priorities, objectives, and values.

(continued)

(*continued*)

The way you handle objections says a lot about you. If you become defensive or combative, if you take it personally, or if you ignore the issue, chances are that any objections will quickly lead to a final rejection, and you will have lost that customer, not just for this one deal but for life. If, on the other hand, you treat objections as opportunities to learn more about your customer, you can work together to find solutions that mitigate concerns and ultimately close this deal or possibly the next deal. When you can do that, you open the door to long-term relationships that will benefit you, your customer, and both of your organizations for years to come.

Work through Objections

How you handle objections says a lot about you. Our research shows that sales reps handle objections in a variety of ways. The most common is to instantly counter with additional information and present features and benefits in an attempt to overcome the customer's concerns. This is not an approach we advise.

When a sales rep tosses out a bunch of features and benefits in response to hearing an objection, that sales rep is essentially telling his customer that she's got it all wrong or that she has misunderstood something. As a result, chances are the customer will simply clam up and tune out whatever is said next. She might well become frustrated or defensive, which does no good when it comes to building rapport and earning trust. Countering an objection by immediately volleying with features and benefits often simply leads to a vicious circle of objections versus benefits. When this happens, the likelihood of overcoming the customer's concerns is decreased.

Instead of entering into an argument with your customer about objections and benefits, it is important to stay neutral and be patient.

Do what you can to diffuse any tension that might surround the objection and show your customer that you are putting her needs first. To this end, our research shows that instead of becoming combative, top-performing sales professionals do what they can to project calm and confidence, avoid confrontation and chaos, and continue to engage the customer in an open conversation. In doing so, they use four critical skills:

- Empathize
- Understand
- Address
- Confirm

Empathize

There is power in empathy—as long as it's genuine. True empathy tells your customer that you heard her objection, are willing to listen to her concerns, and understand where she's coming from. Fake, insincere, or affected empathy is easily detected by your customer and can easily backfire, eroding all the rapport, credibility, and trust you've worked so hard to engender.

Some sales reps are afraid to show empathy because they fear it indicates agreement with their customers. They don't necessarily want to give the impression that they agree with the customer's concern that, say, the tailored solution they've offered is too complex. But empathy isn't about agreement. It simply indicates that you're willing to hear the customer's objections and to consider her point of view. In demonstrating empathy, you need not say, "You're right, Jane: Product X is really complex." Instead, the key is to keep the tone of the conversation in check while making it clear that you understand the customer's objection and that you respect her opinion. So instead of agreeing with her, you can empathize with her by saying something similar to, "I understand that the complexity of the product is an important consideration for you."

Tone here is just as critical as language. This speaks again to the fact that how you say something says as much as what you say. Because it can be easy to become defensive in the face of objections, it's important to slow down and diffuse any tension that surrounds the conversation. Be respectful. Politely show respect toward the customer's objection and let her know that you are ready to listen to her in order to find out where the objection is coming from. The approach here isn't about telling the customer why her objection is unwarranted or insignificant; it's about opening up a path to discovering where the objection stems from.

Remember that objections rarely come out of the blue. There's typically something important behind an objection that's driving the customer's decision. In empathizing with the customer, you can turn an objection into an opportunity to dig deeper and discover what it is that really concerns your customer.

For instance, your customer might raise an objection about the time line for product delivery. She might say, "Well, Product X might work well enough for us, but it just doesn't seem that you can get it to us when we really need it."

The average sales rep might see this as a chance to respond with a recitation of features and benefits in order to reiterate how well the product itself might suit the customer's needs. But top performers take a moment to consider what the customer is really saying and to show some empathy. So instead of volleying with a bunch of specs and data, a top performer would say something along the lines of, "I'm glad to hear that Product X seems as though it might be a good fit for you, and I understand that timely delivery is of utmost importance to you."

Demonstrating some empathy keeps the conversation going, while being combative could shut it down. Empathy opens the door to understanding the core issue so that you can address it properly.

Understand

Countering an objection with features and benefits and specs and data is a natural response and usually a well-intentioned one. It's typical to want to overcome objections by providing information that might sway the customer and convince her that the solution you've presented is exactly right for her.

But when we fail to seek to understand what's driving the customer's objection, we miss an opportunity to learn more about the customer and what's important to her. By volleying with information, we run the risk of making assumptions about what really concerns the customer. When we make assumptions, it can be easy to jump to conclusions in a clumsy attempt to resolve the objection. And in doing so, we can all too easily address the wrong problem or address the concern incompletely. This is what happens when we don't understand what's really bothering the customer.

Customers might object for any number of reasons. But no matter what words they use, it's the sentiment behind the objection that really matters. Your customer might say something along the lines of, "Product X looks really great, but the timing isn't really right for us." But what does that mean?

Your job isn't to respond with a list of features and benefits to shore up the solution you've presented. It's to find out what is really behind your customer's objection. It's important that you understand what's driving the objection so that you can address the real issue. Given that, you might say, "I understand that it's important to make a decision at the right time. If you don't mind me asking, what concerns do you have about the timing?"

An open-ended question such as this prompts further discussion. It serves as a gentle reminder that you are a trusted advisor, one who is willing to listen to his customer so that he can provide counsel. Getting your customer to open up a bit might reveal that the issue isn't so much about timing but about a lack of staff to successfully implement the new product. Further exploration might reveal, for example, that your customer is in the midst of a hiring process that's taking longer than expected, which means that she needs more time before implementing the solution you have advocated.

You might or might not be able to address your customer's concerns and overcome her real objections. But if you don't ask, you'll never understand what's behind them. By empathizing with your customer and seeking to understand the core issue, you can strive to change her perception. You can help her talk through her needs and work through the objection. Only then can you hope to address the issue.

Address

Average sales reps jump straight to this point without empathizing with their customers or understanding the real issues driving the objections. But if you don't understand what's behind the objection, there's really no way to effectively address it.

A trusted advisor seeks to overcome an objection only after striving to understand what the core issue is. Once you understand what the real issue is, you have to ask yourself whether you can actually overcome the objection and satisfy your customer's needs. Either you can or you can't.

If you can satisfy the customer's need, explain how you can do so. This will be the time to highlight those features and benefits that will meet the customer's needs. But be sure to address only those features and benefits that are relevant to the specific objection in question. Don't overwhelm your customer with a recitation of all the specs and data about your product or service. Explain precisely which features and benefits apply to the customer's objection, why they matter, and how they will address her concerns.

Of course, you might not be able to overcome some objections. Your customer might demand an unrealistic delivery schedule, a price you can't match, or a level of service you can't provide. If that's the case, it's important to acknowledge the fact that you can't meet that need—but it's also important to reframe the conversation, focusing on the needs that you can meet with the solution you've tailored for your customer and examining where on the customer's list of priorities this unmet need falls.

In dealing with a need you can't meet, focus on what can be done rather than on what can't be done. Help your customer see the big picture, highlighting the ways in which the solution you have presented meets so many of the customer's other needs, priorities, and objectives. Explore with her the importance of the objection she's raised. You might find that, in actuality, it's a nice-to-have-issue rather than a need-to-have issue.

Don't get hung up on what you can't do, and don't give up on the sale too early. This requires some patience and finesse, keeping your own emotions in check while discussing the issue with your customer. You don't want to push your customer. Rather, it's important to discuss the issue with her, ask questions so that you really understand what the core issue is, and then address the objection—explaining how you can satisfy the need—or refocus the conversation on the big picture.

Confirm

As throughout the rest of the Critical Selling framework, it's important when working through objections and addressing the core issues surrounding them to confirm with your customer that you're on the same page. It is a risky and outright dangerous move to assume that the information you provided alleviated her concern. Unlike when you seek to understand the core issue behind your customer's objection, where you would ask an open-ended question, here you should ask a closed-ended question to confirm. You might say, for instance, "Now that we've discussed how Product X can be rolled out in phases, does that address your concerns about timing?" This is important because you want to ensure that you get a direct response and that you have completely addressed her concern before moving on.

If you get a positive response, it's time to move on in the process. If, however, some lingering objections remain, keep asking questions. Return to the Land of Discovery and dig deeper into the issues. Take the time to address all the questions and concerns your customer has.

Once all questions have been answered and objections resolved, confirm agreement again. Asking a question such as, "Now that we've come up with an alternative solution, does that address your concerns?" gives your customer one more chance to voice her agreement so that you can move forward together as partners in finalizing the purchasing decision.

Of course, objections might come up at any point in the process, not just at closing. The key is to address them promptly, directly, politely, and thoroughly—and then return to wherever you were in the process. If your customer airs concerns during the discovering stage, be grateful that she is giving you an opportunity to address her concerns rather than being silent. Ask questions to get to the heart of the issue and use the information you gain from the discussion to frame how your solution addresses her needs. If that addresses her concern, you can then continue on wherever you were in the sales process before the customer voiced her concern. If objections don't pop up until you're in the midst of closing the deal, you take the same approach, work through the four critical skills, and, once the concern is satisfied, go back to where you were.

Remember, too, that customers sometimes object for reasons they can't even fully articulate. Customers often have hidden needs that even they don't fully understand. Work with them to uncover what's at the heart of their concerns. You will notice that many objections are vague in nature and need some exploring in order to truly understand what the concern is and where it's coming from.

Of course, you might address each and every one of your customer's objections and still not win her business—for any number of reasons. Keep in mind, though, that by following the Critical Selling framework, you are more likely to close the deal, and to close it more quickly and with fewer objections. Also remember, however, that it's not always about this particular sale on this very day with this specific customer. You're in this for the long haul.

As you've worked through the process, you've done what you can to connect with your customer, build rapport, and earn her trust. As a trusted advisor, you've consulted with your customer in order to provide her with a solution uniquely tailored to meet her needs—and to work with her best interests in mind. Your goal is to address her concerns and move forward in the process. But if she doesn't, do whatever you can to maintain goodwill, because today's prospect might well be tomorrow's customer.

Critical Moment: Address Price Objections

In Chapter 5, we talked a bit about handling early price requests. There we looked at how to tactfully delay the price discussion and why it's useful to share with the customer a price range while seeking to discover additional information that can help you better frame the price discussion. Of course, there does come a point at which the price discussion must be had and can no longer be delayed. At some point, you'll have to deal directly with price.

Price is without a doubt one of the biggest stumbling blocks when it comes to closing a deal. In today's hypercompetitive global marketplace, savvy customers know what they want and often have an idea of what something should cost, whether a product or a service. It can be challenging to deal with price objections, but there are a few critical steps sales professionals can take to mitigate concerns about cost.

- **Compare Apples to Apples.** Price is relative to the value perceived by your customer. Your customer might well be talking to sales reps at other companies about a similar product or service, and it's likely he's done a lot of research into the features and benefits that you and your competition offer. It's important that you, too, have a big-picture view of where in the value spectrum your product or service sits, so that you can easily justify the pricing you offer your customer. Don't be afraid to ask your customer what he's comparing your price to: Which product is he looking at? What is included in the competitor's service guarantee? Are they asking for a one-year commitment or longer? Explore the competitive deal with your customer so that you can be sure he's comparing apples to apples and that he understands the full value of your product or service.

(continued)

(continued)

- **Emphasize Value.** Sometimes customers are solely focused on price. The figure attached to the dollar sign is all they can see, and the purchase decision is motivated primarily by the bottom line. In such instances, it can be tempting to immediately adjust your price downward in the hope of closing the deal. But that's not your only option. Look for ways you can be creative about enhancing the value of your product or service relative to the customer's needs. If, for instance, you know through the discovering process that another of his key priorities is efficiency, emphasize how your product can both save time and accelerate growth for his organization. Show him how the cost of the product will pay for itself in a matter of weeks or months—more quickly than any competing products can. Negotiating on price need not always be your first approach; emphasizing value might convince your customer that the price you've offered for the tailored solution you have presented makes sense. Remember that customers often are willing to pay more for a product or service that they believe is better than what the competition is offering.

- **Add Value.** Sometimes the price of a product or service comes with some hidden intangibles the customer might not be aware of. When handling price objections, consider whether adding perks might sway your customer without forcing you to negotiate downward on price. You might, for instance, toss in to the deal VIP status that provides your customer with fast-tracked service or special offers. You might provide additional value for him in the form of enhanced support, one-on-one training, or customized terms. When you can provide your customer with perks that make him feel that he's getting something special, that becomes a unique selling proposition that may well make price less of an objection.

When dealing with price objections, it's critical to avoid commoditizing your product or service by instantly negotiating downward—especially if you're not the low-price leader in your category. Immediately negotiating on price may well give your customer the impression that your product or service was overpriced to begin with, which might end up eroding some of the trust you've built with him. Instead, explore with your customer the true concerns behind his objection to the price. Remember that price need not be your only negotiating tool, and so after making sure your customer is comparing apples to apples, look for ways to emphasize and/or add value so that your customer can see beyond dollar signs and bottom lines.

Maintain Goodwill and Ask for Feedback

The sales process can be fraught with emotion. Customers might feel pressured by organizational demands, schedules, budgets, and so on. So, too, might sales professionals feel the pressure of sales goals and quotas, deadlines, and other performance measures. With competing interests and individual agendas at play, it's important to keep in mind that emotions can sometimes overtake logic during the sales process. But that doesn't translate into a green light to throw professionalism out the window.

Regardless of when a customer voices objections—or the tone or volume in which she does so—it's important to communicate your points clearly and concisely as well as politely and professionally. Whether she raises one objection or a dozen, and even if she delivers a final no, it's important to maintain goodwill. Remember that in dealing with objections, it's important to do nothing that might jeopardize the trust you've earned with your customer.

Despite your best efforts, you might well make a great presentation and get deep into the closing phase of the process only to hear a game-changing objection from your customer. She might raise any number of seemingly insurmountable objections. She might even indicate that she doesn't want to move ahead at all with the solution you have recommended.

It can be all too easy in such a situation to become defensive or to take objections as personal or professional rejection. Keep in mind, though, the importance of maintaining a positive impression with your customer. Remember that you might not close this deal but that you could well have other successful business dealings with this customer in the future. How you handle objections might affect your customer's perception of you and your organization, enhancing or hampering your ability to work together in the future.

When you have exhausted all opportunities and the customer indicates that the deal is dead, be sure to thank the customer for taking the time to speak with you, to discuss her needs, and for sharing with you the details of the situation that brought you together in the first place. Let her know how important she is to you and your organization and that, despite any objections she has raised, you will be available in the future to help her whenever you can. Doing so reminds your customer that your conversation hasn't been just about selling a particular widget to her, but that it has been about consulting with and advising her in the hopes of coming together on a mutually beneficial solution. No matter how disappointed you might be, there's no reason to destroy the confidence your customer has in you, the rapport you have shared, or the trust you've earned. Do what you can to maintain goodwill.

Do also what you can to turn a "no" into a learning opportunity. Take the time to ask for feedback in order to learn why you didn't win the business this time. If the final answer is no, ask your customer if she would be willing to share with you the factors that contributed to her decision. Ask her to discuss anything lacking in the product or service you offered and how that affected her perception of the solution you recommended. Ask if there was anything you did or did not do that influenced her decision.

Remember that asking for feedback should by no means feel as though you're pressuring your customer or attempting to change her mind. Now is not the time to go for the hard sell. Instead, now is the time to maintain goodwill and look to the future. The feedback you gain during this discussion can help you carry on a productive, ongoing relationship with the customer.

No one likes getting negative feedback. It's no fun to hear "no" from your customers. But it's critical not to take objections personally, instead handling them professionally and with empathy. Top-performing sales professionals understand that overcoming objections requires them to ask questions and listen attentively—just as they have done throughout the entire selling conversation.

When you take the time to work with your customer to get to the bottom of each of her objections, you are in a better position to maintain the kind of goodwill that helps you close the deal. That keeps you in good stead as a trusted advisor with your customer, sealing your reputation as a top-performing sales professional who has his customers' interests at heart—the kind of sales pro your customers are happy to recommend again and again.

Critical Selling: Lessons Learned

- Although objections are a natural part of the sales process, top performers understand how real objections sound, why objections arise, and how to reduce the number of objections they receive by handling the sales process effectively.
- Top-performing sales professionals take the time to think through potential objections ahead of time and outline how they might address them so they are best prepared to deal with objections at any point during the sales process. Anticipating objections and planning for them are critical skills top performers use regularly.
- When it comes to handling objections and dealing with rejection, top performers know that mindset matters. By considering objections to be opportunities to gain further insight into their

customers, top performers are better able to avoid becoming defensive or combative. They know that objections aren't personal; rather, they are opportunities to understand and to further build trust with their customers.

- Top performers use four critical skills—empathize, understand, address, and confirm—to get to the heart of each and every objection. It's important to show customers you respect the objections they have raised and to seek information that will help you understand and address the issues that lie at the heart of those objections. Once you've gained a handle on the root cause of the objection and determined whether and how you can address it, it's crucial to confirm that you and your customer are on the same page so that you can move forward together.

- In sales, no matter how effective you are, you will inevitably lose a few. In those situations, top performers understand the importance of maintaining goodwill and asking for feedback. They use the opportunity to understand why they didn't win the business and what they could do next time to get a better outcome.

Conclusion
Putting It All Together:
Mindset + Practice + Process + Action

WHEN IT COMES to sales, there are a lot of ways to improve performance. Our research has shown us, time and time again, that the Critical Selling framework we've shared with you in these pages is a highly effective way for sales professionals to accelerate the sales process, reduce the number of objections, and close more deals. Sales reps at companies large and small—from Cartier, HSBC, Philips, Cummins, Broadridge, and Wells Fargo to Freeway Insurance, Scratch Events, Enartis Vinquiry, National Motor Club, and InfinityQS—and across a number of industries (whether business and professional services or consumer goods and retail or energy and utilities) have benefited from following these critical steps throughout each and every sales interaction.

From planning to opening to discovering to presenting to closing, top-performing sales professionals understand how critical it is to implement each of these steps, every time, with every customer. They accept the need to change, adopt a positive mindset, and adapt their behavior in order to keep up with ever-more-savvy customers in a fiercely competitive, global, and 24/7 marketplace. They continue to practice, to hone their skills, and to keep up with training, regardless of how much tenure they possess or how much success they have enjoyed in the past.

They do this because, as we've mentioned, research indicates that much of the purchase decision-making process is already underway before customers connect with sales professionals. Some studies note that as many as 94 percent of buyers conduct some form of online research before purchasing a business product.[1] In addition, some reports note that "67 percent of the buyer's journey is now done digitally" and that most executives start their purchasing journey with an online search into readily available information.[2] Top performers keep practicing because they know they have less time to do more work with customers who are already a step ahead.

In the face of what some people might consider to be a rather large shift in buying behavior, practicing your skills in order to improve sales performance has never been more important. Also critical is to follow the steps we've discussed in these pages—all the steps, from beginning to end. We've said it before, but it bears repeating: the Critical Selling framework is not a buffet. If you want to become a top-performing sales professional, you have to plan. You have to connect with your customers. You have to ask questions (and listen to the answers). You have to meet customers where they are in their buying journey. And, perhaps most important, you have to commit to the process by adopting a positive mindset and a willingness to change your behavior.

Plan Each Sales Interaction

We talked a lot about planning in Chapter 3, examining the importance of planning ahead when connecting with customers, from the initial call throughout the process to closing and beyond. When most of today's customers have already done their homework—looking into you, your product or service, and your organization, as well as your competition—it's critical to plan accordingly.

Sales reps who launch into their spiel without accounting for this fact will quickly find it difficult to engage with their customers in a meaningful way. Top performers understand the importance of planning for each phase of the Critical Selling framework and for each and every customer interaction.

Planning goes well beyond conducting some research on your customers in advance of your initial contact with them, although that is an important part of the process. It is, of course, crucial to plan for your opening, for discovering, for presenting, and for closing. Planning is critical to the entire Critical Selling framework.

In Chapter 3, we shared a precall planner form (see Figure 3.2) that many top-performing sales professionals find useful. Whether you use this form or one like it, or whether you simply jot down some thoughts on a piece of paper or your mobile device, planning is crucial. It's important to make a note of whom you will talk to, what you will talk about, what you hope to achieve during each conversation, how you will follow up after each call, and so on and so forth.

With that, a critical part of planning includes setting objectives that are specific, appropriate, and measurable. As we have discussed, SAM objectives help you clearly identify what you want to accomplish so that you can build an approach that will help you get there. Setting such objectives helps you focus each of your customer interactions so that you can use your time—and your customer's time—wisely, ensuring that you tackle all the important issues you both want to cover. Without planning, it's all too easy to lose focus, get sidetracked, and suddenly discover that your selling conversation has been derailed and, as a result, ended up being inefficient. This isn't good for you or for your customer, and it's no way to build the kind of credibility that will help you become a trusted advisor.

Also important when it comes to planning is to think about how you will approach each customer. For the initial call, some research into your prospect, her organization, and her industry will provide you with crucial insight that will help you plan for that conversation. In subsequent dealings, think about the approach you will take.

Take into consideration your customer's style. Is she friendly and personable? Business oriented? A visionary? Cautious and skeptical? How will your customer's style affect how you interact with her? Plan your approach based on what's best for your customer.

As your conversations progress through opening and discovering, planning also will help you prepare for the presenting phase of the Critical Selling framework. In fact, planning here is critical. Why? Because a carefully planned presentation will allow you to share with your customer a solution uniquely tailored to her needs, goals, priorities, and values.

As we discussed in Chapter 6, planning a presentation personalized for your customer is critical. Customers don't want to sit through the same canned presentation that they know (and you know) everyone else got, too. Planning helps you highlight the specific ways in which your product or solution will meet your customer's unique needs. It ensures that you discuss key points; that you accurately report data, specs, features, and benefits; and that you emphasize the information that is most relevant to your customer. On the other hand, winging it—that is, not planning—almost certainly guarantees that you'll forget to discuss critical information, whether because it slips your mind, because your customer derails you with an interruption, or because you run out of time.

Of course, all the planning in the world does little good if you don't also reflect on what you've learned during each sales interaction. Our research indicates that top performers take time not only to plan ahead but also to reflect after each customer interaction. They take notes during each call, and they jot down their thoughts afterward. Doing so provides valuable information and insight that can be helpful during future customer conversations. Planning and reflecting are part of a virtuous circle: without planning, a sales call could be unproductive; without reflecting, it's difficult to plan for the next call.

Top performers make it a practice to plan for each selling conversation, from initial call all the way through closing. They understand the risks of not planning, instead taking the time to think about how to best approach each customer and what to focus on during each call. By doing so, they not only maximize their time but also better connect with their customers.

Connect and Reconnect

When you get down to it, sales is very much about the relationship between you and your customer—not about challenging or confronting your customer but about connecting. Products and services are important, too, of course, but although features and benefits vary from one provider to another, they're often quite similar, and sometimes the discernible differences can be negligible. As a result, success in sales often boils down to how well you connect with your customers.

Throughout these pages, we've discussed the importance of connecting with your customers—finding common ground, establishing like interests, and building rapport, as well as staying in touch. In Chapter 4, for example, we looked at ways to connect with your customer in order to set the stage for a solid opening. Connecting with your customer doesn't end once you've opened the sales interaction well, though; connecting with your customer is something you do throughout the sales interaction, from opening to discovering to presenting to closing—and beyond.

Connecting with your customer helps you establish rapport, build credibility, and earn trust. It helps you discover critical information about your customer that you can use to tailor a unique solution that meets his needs, sharing relevant data, features, and benefits about that solution in a winning presentation. And it helps you accelerate the sales process and close more deals.

Top-performing sales professionals make it a habit to practice connecting with their customers. They research their customers in order to find unique and differentiated ways in which they can establish rapport. They make a practice of asking questions and actively listening to the answers. They continually ask for feedback.

They confirm understanding with their customers before moving forward. They find ways to keep in touch and stay front-of-mind with their customers.

Keeping in touch with your customers might take any number of forms. Phone calls, e-mails, and face-to-face meetings are typical ways to stay in contact. Top performers use these methods and others to stay connected. Articles, blog posts, newsletters, and white papers also help sales reps connect with their customers. Engaging in conversations on social media venues such as Facebook, Twitter, and LinkedIn also keep customers and sales reps connected, as well. All of these approaches can be effective ways to let your customers know that you're thinking about them and that you're interested in the issues that concern them. It's important to keep up with this. Practice making it a habit to stay in touch with your customers.

Of course, connecting with your customers isn't just about what you do; it's also about how you do it. The method you use should be the one that is the most effective at that stage of the sales process and also the most likely to resonate with your customer. Whatever approach you take, you should keep these two things in mind. It is important not only to let your customers know that you're thinking about them but also to do so in a way that makes them feel comfortable.

Just as important as the medium is the message—what you say and how you say it. When connecting with your customers, keep in mind their communication style. Make sure your vocal presence is n sync. And, as we discussed in Chapter 6, use the customer's own words when talking with him. Repeating his key words and phrases can be a powerful way to connect: it shows your customer that you have been listening to him and that his concerns have been heard. (We'll talk more below about the importance of listening.)

Of course, the connections you make with your customers should stretch well beyond the selling conversation. Our research reveals that one major, common mistake that typical sales reps make is disconnecting with customers if they don't get the sale, dropping the customer like a hot potato after hearing that final no. Top performers, on the other hand, understand the importance of staying connected, regardless of whether the deal is closed.

Part of the reason for this is that once you've established rapport, built credibility, and earned trust, it's easier and more efficacious to stay connected than to have to reconnect and start all over again—trying to build rapport, credibility, and trust a second time. Staying connected provides opportunities to discuss other needs your customer might have, or needs that his colleagues, friends, and peers might have. It keeps you front-of-mind so that if and when he's ready to purchase again, you're the one he turns to first.

In fact, connecting and reconnecting with your customers provides myriad benefits, both tangible and intangible. Top performers practice staying in touch with customers through different avenues of communication, keeping themselves front-of-mind by sharing news and information of interest to their customers. They also practice finding ways to connect with their customers on a visceral level, finding areas of common ground and common interest in order to build rapport.

Ask Questions (and Listen to the Answers)

One of the key tools top-performing sales professionals keep in their arsenal is the question. Asking the right questions at the right time in the right manner of the right individual can be a powerful tool when it comes to accelerating the sales process and closing more deals. Top performers practice making the most of this critical component of successful selling.

We've talked a lot in these pages about asking questions. In Chapter 5, for instance, we discussed the importance of asking open-ended questions during the discovering phase of the Critical Selling framework. Open-ended questions do much to help you learn about your customers' needs, goals, priorities, and values. Asking such questions (and listening to the answers) not only helps you gain priceless information about your customers and how you can meet their needs but also further positions you as a real person who is truly interested in hearing what your customers have to say—which speaks to your position as a trusted advisor, not just an order taker intent on making a sale.

As we've noted, our research tells us that when you ask the right questions in the right ways, your customers will tell you exactly how and what to sell to them. The challenge, of course, is in asking questions that are, in fact, the right questions. A lot of sales reps pepper their customers with quick, closed-ended, yes-no questions designed to lead to a specific outcome. This approach rarely works and does not drive the deal toward a win. It does little to position you as a knowledgeable, credible expert to whom your customers can turn again and again for valuable advice. Instead, asking open-ended questions leads to information that is much more revealing. Questions that begin with "what," "where," "which," "who," "why," "how," "tell me about . . ." and the like prompt your customers to confide in you, sharing their current situation, their desired outcome, and what it will take to get from one to the other.

Of course, you can't just run through a generic checklist of open-ended questions, moving from one to the next as soon as you hear an answer you like. That's not how it works. Instead, it's critical to listen to the answers. Pay attention so that you can ask any appropriate follow-up questions. Ask for clarification if needed. Make it clear to your customer that you really want to discuss his needs and goals with him. This will further cement in his mind your concern for him and his organization and your willingness to help him meet his objectives—rather than your desire to make a sale.

Listening to your customers is critical if you want to connect with them. By asking questions and actively listening to the answers, you will go far not only in gathering important information that will help you close the deal with fewer objections but also in building credibility and earning trust. As we've mentioned, listening may, in fact, "be the single most important skill that salespeople can possess."[3] In addition, as noted earlier, "customers' perceptions of the quality of salespeople's listening [skills] were found to be positively related to customers' trust in salespeople, their satisfaction with them, and their desire to do future business with them."[4] Remember, too, that failure to listen is one of the most important inhibitors to successful selling.[5]

Top performers regularly practice good listening skills so that they can better connect with their customers. Researching your customers, asking good questions, keeping in touch—none of that matters if you don't listen to your customers' responses. Listening is critical when it comes to connecting with customers, whether for the first time or the hundredth, whether at opening or at closing, whether you get the sale or not.

As you move through each selling conversation, it's critical to keep asking questions, to ask for clarification, to ask for feedback, and to ask for confirmation. We discussed asking for feedback in Chapter 6 during our look at best practices for presenting tailored solutions to your customers. In Chapter 7, we looked at the importance of asking for confirmation at closing, making sure that your customer understands and is ready for the next steps as you move from suggesting a solution to advocating for one. We also talked about the importance of, when the moment is right, asking your customer for his business.

"Ask and ye shall receive."

Note that this old adage isn't "Talk a lot and ye shall receive" or "Make it all about you and ye shall receive." Asking is what makes things happen. Top-performing sales reps understand that there is power in asking, not least of which because it furthers each sales interaction; but also because it allows you to identify not only known needs but also unknown needs of the customer. Asking questions assures the customer that the selling conversation is about him, discovering what he needs, and finding out what will help meet those needs. The selling conversation isn't about you as the sales rep touting your experience, or expertise, or the quality of your product or service, or the superiority of your organization. It's not about overtly trying to convince your customer that what you can offer him is the best option. It's about asking the right questions in the right manner so that together you can discuss what's best for your customer.

Top performers understand the importance of practicing the art of asking questions and actively listening to the answers. They make a point of incorporating open-ended questions into each phase of the sales process and of using closed-ended questions at key junctures in order to secure agreement from their customers. They're not afraid of asking for feedback and for confirmation. In fact, top performers aren't afraid of much when it comes to sales and selling.

Critical Moment: Don't Forget the "Don'ts"

When mastering the skills, strategies, and best practices that will become fundamental to your ongoing career as a top-performing sales professional, there are a lot of things to keep track of—new approaches to try out, new methods to practice, new ways of thinking to adopt. But there are also a lot of things you shouldn't be doing. Here are some common pitfalls you should avoid.

- **Don't Try to Pick and Choose from among the Phases in the Framework.** It's a process, not a buffet. Top performers understand the value of following all the steps, every time, with every customer. Each step, no matter how small, plays an important role in your overall selling success.
- **Don't Assume That Each of Your Customers Already Considers You a Trusted Advisor.** Know where you fall on the Relationship Continuum with each of your customers so that you can focus on the skills that will help you grow each relationship.
- **Don't Skip Planning for Each Selling Conversation.** Prepare for each sales interaction with a little planning. Think about whom you'll be talking to, what the issues are, what the objectives are, and how you want to achieve them. Don't go blind into any sales call thinking you can just wing it.

- **Don't Forget to Reflect.** After each sales interaction, take a few minutes to jot down some notes about what you've learned—and do it as soon as possible after the call. Don't waste what you've learned by hoping you'll remember it later.

- **Don't Think That One Size Fits All.** Tailor your approach to each of your customers during each phase of the sales process, making sure you're in sync with their individual communication styles and where they are in the buying process, and that you're discussing what's important to them—not just what's important to you.

- **Don't Interrogate Your Customers.** It's important to ask your customers targeted questions in order to understand their needs, but don't barrage them with a list of pointed questions so they feel as though they're being interrogated. Keep it conversational—focused and friendly, not pushy or probing.

- **Don't Go in for the Close before It's Time to Close.** It's critical to follow the process. There's no need to rush your customer, to pressure her, or to cajole her into buying your product or service. Take the time to build rapport and earn her trust. Don't rush the process, and don't think that you have to always be closing.

- **Don't Fear Objections.** Instead of looking at objections as a sign of doom, consider them opportunities instead—opportunities to learn more about your customer, to help her see how your product or service can meet her needs, to further discuss issues that are important to her.

Top-performing sales professionals don't look for ways to cut corners. They understand that by following the process and going through each phase of the framework, every time

(continued)

(*continued*)

with every customer, they will accelerate the sales process and close more deals. There's no reason to rush a sale; the process takes care of itself, leading naturally to a mutually beneficial close.

Adjust Your Attitude

If it's true that top-performing sales professionals aren't afraid to ask questions (and our research tells us as much), that fearlessness has a lot to do with attitude. In fact, attitude has a lot to do with success in general.

Throughout these pages, we've talked about the importance of a positive attitude. In Chapter 2, we focused on the importance of adopting an open and growing mindset when it comes to embracing the kind of change required to follow through with each and every phase of the Critical Selling framework. Attitude is crucial when it comes to implementing change, because not only are most of us reluctant to change in the first place but also we need to understand, accept, and believe in the changes that face us. If we don't open our minds to change, if we're not willing to shift our attitudes, if we won't commit to altering our behavior—well, then, change isn't going to happen.

In essence, most of us take a "what's in it for me?" attitude to change. Most of us weigh the costs and benefits of change against the costs and benefits of maintaining the status quo,[6] and if the perceived impact of change isn't in our favor—well, then, again, change isn't going to happen.

Top performers, however, are open to change. They're confident that change will benefit them and their organizations. They're willing to try new things to improve their performance. They're open to the idea of changing their behavior in order to see better results from their efforts. They're inclined toward lifelong learning, continuing education, and ongoing training. They're willing to practice, practice, practice—doing whatever it takes to gain that edge.

This attitude is critical when it comes to improving sales performance. Sales isn't about talent or luck. It's not just about how many hours you put in or how much effort you expend. Nor is it just about how many customers you call on. It's about practicing, training, and applying proven methods designed to help you close more deals.

Changing times require new processes, and today's savvy customers have different expectations than they did even just a few years ago. The pace of change is so fast that if you cling to yesterday's methodologies, you're going to get run over.

What we're talking about is what it takes to become a top performer who connects with customers and becomes a trusted advisor. Top-performing sales professionals are those who are willing to learn new skills and strategies, to train, and to practice so that they can have successful sales interactions with today's customers.

We're not asking you to become someone else. We're not insisting that you buy in to a cult of personality. What we are suggesting is that it will be easier for you to change your behavior for the better not only when you understand how doing so will benefit you but also when you open your mind to adopting the intuitive strategies, skills, and best practices that our research tells us works. Our research also tells us that practice is important, that working on skills is valuable, and that top performers fully understand the need to continue evolving if they want to be the best.

Most of us tend to resist change. We tend to feel that we already know what we need to know, especially if we're tenured professionals who have chalked up a few successes during our careers. But if in 2016 you're selling the way you did in 1996, or even 2006, chances are you've developed some bad habits that could be improved upon. And if that's the case, it's probably time to change.

Is it time for you to think about embracing the kind of change that will help you improve your performance? Let's see.

Take a look at the list below. Think about each item and consider whether you agree or disagree. Be honest with yourself (no one else has to see this but you!).

- Meeting or exceeding my sales performance measures is as easy as it's ever been.
- When I lose a sale, it's usually because the customer didn't understand what my product or service could do for him.
- Customers are essentially the same as they've always been.
- I don't have the time to ask my customers too many questions before telling them about my product or service.
- It's important to be assertive with my customers.
- I can usually assume that I know what my customers need.
- My regular presentation works just fine for all my customers.
- It's never too soon to ask my customer for his business and close the deal.
- What my competitors are doing matters less to me and my customers than what my own organization is doing.
- Being a friendly, personable sales rep is the most important thing I can be for my customers.
- I don't have time to attend training workshops and seminars.
- I've honed my approach into a reliable one that works with all my customers.

If you found yourself agreeing with these statements more than you disagreed, it's likely time for a shift in attitude and behavior. Why? Because each of these statements speaks to the kind of outmoded thinking that leaves sales reps mired in the status quo, while those around them are moving ahead and keeping up with the pace of change—and with their customers.

Are you ready to do what it takes to keep up with the pace of change? Are you ready to establish credibility with your customers so that they see you as a trusted advisor they can turn to again and again? Are you ready to rethink how you open your sales calls? Are you ready to use new skills to discover more about your customers? Are you ready to employ proven strategies to present tailor-made solutions that meet your customers' needs? Are you ready to work with your customer toward a natural close?

We hope so. Because ready or not, change is coming. Whether you're willing and able to keep pace with the changes that are shaking the world of sales and selling is entirely up to you. If you want to become a top-performing sales professional, if you want to accelerate the sales process and close more deals with fewer objections, it's critical that you adopt a positive mindset; embrace change; seek out training; and keep practicing the skills, strategies, and best practices that will position you as a trusted advisor with all your customers for years to come.

Critical Moment: Commit to Change and Take Action

How do you eat an elephant? One bite at a time.

That well-worn analogy is an apt one when it comes to embracing change. We understand that change can be daunting. Trying to rework your entire approach to sales can seem overwhelming.

So don't do it. Don't try to rework your entire approach. At least not all at once.

We want you to be open to change. We want you to commit to being the best you can be. We want you to commit to following the Critical Selling framework so that you can accelerate the sales process and close more deals while connecting with your customers and earning their trust.

But that doesn't mean we think you should try to fix everything all at once—or that you even need to fix everything about your approach to sales. You might very well be doing

(*continued*)

(*continued*)

great at some things and just need to tweak some others. A little bit of change can mean big results if you work on the right things.

Big changes are the result of a lot of little steps. So instead of trying to completely turn around every aspect of your sales approach, commit instead to tackling three skills and best practices. Work on these three things until you feel that you've got them down. Then tackle three more. And so on.

So take a look at this list and check off the three items that you want to focus on first:

- Identify where on the Relationship Continuum I'm situated with each of my customers.
- Make it a practice to use the precall planning tool before each and every selling conversation.
- Set SAM objectives for each sales interaction.
- Make it a habit to reflect after each call, using the postcall planning tool or jotting down some notes about each customer.
- Identify the communication style of each of my customers and adapt my approach accordingly.
- Deliver an LPS during the opening of each selling conversation, in e-mails, and in voice mails.
- Work on improving my presence (language, vocal quality, and body language).
- Ask questions that target the six critical areas of focus.
- Actively listen to my customers, seeking clarification or elucidation when needed and confirming understanding before moving on.
- Create engagement with each of my customers by layering in benefits, keeping each call conversational, and adapting my approach to suit the customer.

- Work through early price requests by finding ways to tactfully delay the discussion and/or providing the customer with a price range.
- Present my customers with a solution uniquely tailored to their needs, addressing the needs and objectives they have shared with me.
- Ask my customers for feedback after each and every presentation, gauging how satisfied they are with the solution I have suggested.
- Adjust my communication approach so that I present persuasively, linking my solution to my customer's needs, adjusting my vocal qualities, and repeating the customer's words.
- Strengthen the solution by utilizing social proof, addressing alternative options, and helping customers acknowledge the consequences of their decision.
- Summarize with each customer the conversations we've had as we move toward closing.
- Gain commitment from customers by actively advocating for the solution I've presented and asking them to move forward.
- Define next steps so the customer fully understands what will happen next and who is responsible for what.
- Confirm understanding with the customer during each phase of the sales process before moving on to the next step.
- Accept that objections are part of the process and work on ways to address them in a customer-focused way without being becoming defensive.

Change takes time. In fact, conventional wisdom holds that it takes about 30 days to make or break a habit. Work on the three items you've committed to for the next month or so and

(*continued*)

(*continued*)

assess your progress. When you're confident that your new habits are making a positive difference in your performance, tackle three more. Over time you'll find that your overall performance has improved, leading to accelerating the sales process and closing more deals.

Appendix
Case Study: The McCrone Group

JANEK PERFORMANCE GROUP works with numerous organizations across a variety of industries. Over the years, we've worked with thousands of sales professionals to help them improve their selling acumen so that they can accelerate the sales process and close more deals. Some clients come to us through the various public workshops we offer, while most approach us so that we can work with them directly.

Such was the case with The McCrone Group, a private company founded in 1956, which contacted us in 2010. Based in the Chicago suburbs, The McCrone Group (TMG) is a world leader in the fields of microscopy, microanalysis, materials characterization, instrument sales, and related education. The organization consists of three member companies: McCrone Associates, Inc. (MA), McCrone Microscopes & Accessories, LLC (MMA), and Hooke College of Applied Sciences, LLC (HCAS). In addition, The McCrone Group offers two free online resources: McCroneAtlas.com and ModernMicroscopy.com. For the purposes of this case study, we'll focus on the three core companies: MA, MMA, and HCAS.

McCrone Associates is the oldest of the three TMG companies. MA focuses on solving materials and particle identification problems for a variety of clients from academia, industry, clinical laboratories, government agencies, and scientific researchers. At MA, a team of scientists analyzes various materials and particles, consulting directly with clients and using advanced microscopy techniques and instruments to help solve their clients' problems.

MMA focuses on the sale of instruments including microscopes, digital microscope systems, digital imaging systems, various laboratory supplies, and other technical products. At MMA, technical sales representatives act as trusted advisors to scientists in the field of microscopy.

Hooke College of Applied Sciences provides undergraduate programs in conjunction with other colleges and universities; education and training to scientists worldwide; and professional development courses in such areas as light and electron microscopy, sample preparation, spectroscopy, and image analysis.

Although the individual focuses of each of these businesses vary, they also overlap. All of the offerings provided are related to microscopy and microanalysis. All three businesses have staff members with highly technical backgrounds serving in customer-facing roles. And all three businesses deal with customers whose needs also are focused on microscopy, microanalysis, and related fields. The McCrone Group as a whole wanted to improve sales across the organization; however, the organization essentially approached us from the perspective of three independent businesses, each with unique challenges regarding sales and selling.

The Challenge

Although each of The McCrone Group businesses faced its own unique challenges, several core issues were at the heart at their situation: the businesses needed to work together more efficiently in order to better meet customer needs; as an organization, they needed to better leverage customer relationships; each of the businesses needed to be less reactive and more proactive in order to maximize sales; the entire staff needed to consider themselves not just scientists or technicians but also trusted advisors; and, finally, the organization needed to grow overall sales by reaching more customers and establishing deeper relationships. It was these challenges that ultimately brought The McCrone Group to Janek. Now let's take a look at each business and its unique challenges independently.

McCrone Microscopes & Accessories (MMA)

The technical sales representatives at MMA all came from science-based backgrounds and were primarily tasked to process inbound orders when customers called in to request products featured in MMA's product catalog. As such, they were reactive rather than proactive, and the organization needed everyone in this group to be more customer focused, ask more questions, and make better recommendations for the instruments and equipment in order to better serve their customers. Not doing so was creating missed opportunities—and lost sales—and keeping them farther to the left on The Relationship Continuum than was desired. The primary challenge with MMA was to improve the skill set of their sales staff and teach them to become true trusted advisors to their customers.

McCrone Associates (MA)

MA was comprised of scientists whose jobs included a project management component and who worked directly with clients on a daily basis. The scientists simply didn't see themselves as salespeople, and selling did not come naturally for them. Most were comfortable discussing the scientific portion of a project, and from that standpoint were trusted advisors. However, few had any formal sales training that supported putting them at ease with the "sales" portion of a project and building stronger customer relationships. The MA scientists faced challenges with both skill set and mindset.

Hooke College of Applied Sciences (HCAS)

Similar to the MA side of the business, the team at Hooke College was highly reactive. This group needed to do more outbound business development in order to establish new channels and reach new students. At Hooke College, individuals in administrative positions also acted as registrars, and growing relationships was new to most of them. Less experienced in this area, the team at Hooke College was challenged with gaining the skill set needed to conduct more outreach to potential students and be more proactive.

Because the staff at The McCrone Group tended to be more reactive than proactive, and because most had never gone through any formal sales training, it was difficult for them to move beyond order-taker status to the status of trusted advisor. Think back to our discussion in Chapter 1, in which we discussed the four different and distinct levels of customer relationships that sales professionals can earn. These levels form The Relationship Continuum, which ranges from order taker to friendly salesperson to effective salesperson to, finally, trusted advisor. It's at that trusted-advisor status that top-performing sales professionals are best able to accelerate the sales process, close deals, and grow business (both their own and the businesses of their customers). And it's to trusted-advisor status that The McCrone Group wanted to advance its team of scientists/salespeople.

Leaders at The McCrone Group knew they were experiencing positive year-over-year growth, but they also realized that there was more out there—more clients they could serve and more opportunities they could capture. Furthermore, they recognized that, although they were scientists first, they also were salespeople who worked with customers on a daily basis. As scientists/salespeople, they realized they might not be approaching sales in the right way if they wanted to continue to grow the organization. As a result, the scientists/salespeople were missing opportunities, which precluded them from expanding relationships and getting more business from existing customers. They needed some training—but, first, they needed to change their mindset.

The Solution

In Chapter 2, we looked closely at the importance of having an open mind when looking to adapt new skills, strategies, and best practices designed to help change behavior when seeking improved performance. Mindset matters. This is true regardless of tenure or industry, which is exactly what the professionals at The McCrone Group found.

The mindset at The McCrone Group was along the lines of "we're scientists, not salespeople." There was a teaching-an-old-dog-new-tricks challenge to overcome, particularly in MMA, with tenured sales reps who had become set in their ways.

"We felt that it was important to expose the scientists to some sales techniques," says David Wiley, president of McCrone Associates, "because it's a facet of project management and a facet of initial engagement. Certainly [our scientists] could benefit from some of the tools and knowledge that traditional salespeople use in their approach to clients, understanding needs, and building value."

Recognizing that mindset was an important facet of improving overall performance at The McCrone Group, the solution included a three-pronged approach: prepare and plan, train the team, and sustain the skills.

Prepare and Plan

Janek's professionals worked closely with leaders and staff throughout The McCrone Group in order to understand the company as a whole and its various divisions. Customizing a training program that was specifically tailored to their unique organization was instrumental in The McCrone Group's choice to work with Janek. So, over the course of several days, Janek's team met with key stakeholders during on-site visits, talking with leaders and managers. Janek spoke with individual staff members within each unit and observed live sales interactions. It was important to understand the current state of the organization and the challenges that brought The McCrone Group and Janek together. Together, key stakeholders from both firms worked to identify how scientists/salespeople across MA, MMA, and HCAS were interacting with customers, where the gaps were, and what kind of training was needed for each business. Interviews were held with key stakeholders and managers during an intensive information-gathering process designed to build a tailored sales training experience.

Planning and preparation were critical when it came to letting the scientists/salespeople in each business know that Janek understood where they were coming from, and that Janek understood the need both to become a true sales team and to instill a sales-and-selling mindset across the organization. Also important was using some of the same lingo used by The McCrone Group. For instance, because the scientists at MA saw themselves first as scientists and not so much as salespeople, Janek's team members were careful to recognize the audience for their highly technical expertise and background. This went far in making them feel comfortable and be more open-minded to the training process.

Train the Team

Knowing that MA and MMA, in particular, had different mindsets when it came to sales and selling, Janek wrote unique learning examples for each business and performed various levels of customization for the sales training, which employees would undergo through in-house workshops and other sessions. Janek provided customized training for the scientists/salespeople as well as for leadership and management at The McCrone Group.

Sales Training   Modular training that included hands-on exercises, role-playing scenarios, and interactive examples helped the scientists/salespeople apply lessons learned in true-to-life scenarios. It was important that the training go beyond theory to practical application. So, on-site training took place over the course of a few two-day sessions, providing the scientists/salespeople with real-world skills that could be applied right away.

Leadership Training   In addition, Janek worked with managers and leaders to deliver sales coaching techniques they could use to provide ongoing inspiration and guidance to their staff long after the training sessions had ended. Leaders and managers were instructed in practical tools they could use to build skills, coach effectively, and implement a performance management system that tracked who was being coached, how often, and in what ways.

Sustain the Skills

After the training sessions, during which scientists/salespeople, leaders, and managers were introduced to the Critical Selling skills framework, Janek worked closely with The McCrone Group to identify what the organization needed to do to lead change, reinforce skills, mentor managers, and supplement training. Follow-up was provided in the form of webinars, refresher courses, and ongoing discussions in order to ensure that the lessons learned were implemented and that the associated skills became second nature for both the individuals and for the organization as a whole.

Only once the issue of mindset was addressed could The McCrone Group and Janek work together to craft a solution that would help MA, MMA, and HCAS better meet the needs of their customers, build relationships, and expand their businesses. That solution needed to address The McCrone Group's key issues, which included building long-term relationships, growing the business, and moving the scientists/salespeople to trusted-advisor status, but without sacrificing the scientific and technical expertise required to sell such specialized products and services.

"The products we sell are technical in nature, so there's a level of education that's required in order to sell these products," says Jeff McGinn, president of MMA and HCAS. "So, the whole notion of 'trusted advisor' and how you define that and how you become that for your customers is important when it comes to these highly technical pieces of equipment. We want people to rely on us and come back to us. It's not just about the big sale. It's about forming the relationship and being able to carry it forward, whether it's follow-on sales with accessories, another system they might need, or supporting the purchase they've made. We felt like that was an important part of what we needed to do as an organization, not only to grow, but to do our jobs better."

Implementing the Solution

Every industry is different, and every salesperson is different. It was important that the sales training geared toward The McCrone Group focus on their specific needs, particularly because of their unique mix of scientists/salespeople. As such, every piece of the sales training had some sort of application to what The McCrone Group needed. According to leadership at The McCrone Group, no one came away thinking they got only a couple things out of the entire training and that otherwise it was a waste of time. A modular approach to the training helped employees feel engaged and that their time was well spent.

In addition to customized training workshops, practice sessions also helped The McCrone Group implement the skills and strategies they learned. After learning about new concepts, employees were encouraged to practice new skills and strategies on each other, testing out real-world scenarios together. These practice sessions were conducted in-house before The McCrone Group sales professionals tried out the new skills on their customers, which helped them build their confidence. In addition, because all the employees were from the same company and had similar scientific and technical backgrounds, they all had similar needs and understandings, which made them feel more comfortable about both undergoing training and practicing their newfound skills with each other.

In addition to adopting a sales-and-selling mindset and practicing critical skills and best practices, growing the organization and shifting from order taker to trusted advisor were important to The McCrone Group. They learned to do that by augmenting the conversations they were already having with their clients and customers. Whereas the scientists/salespeople at The McCrone Group had long been having in-depth discussions with customers in order to discern particular needs, they weren't going beyond those initial issues to uncover additional needs. Furthermore, they didn't necessarily consider the conversations they were having as part of an overall discovering process that would help them meet their customers' needs and close more deals.

In recognizing that the scientists/salespeople at The McCrone Group weren't necessarily thinking about discovering as part of an overall sales process, leaders at the company realized that they hadn't even known that they didn't know how to ask the right questions. They hadn't been focused on asking questions to uncover needs or to dig deeper into the customer's values and objectives. They weren't actively undertaking a discovering process that would help them uncover needs.

As a result of the training and practice sessions, the scientists/salespeople quickly came to understand the importance of better customer focused questions. As a result, the scientists/salespeople became better equipped to have meaningful, productive conversations with their customers. They learned how to cater their questions to their clients and how to frame their questions around the unique products and services they offer, as well as around the specialized insight and advice they could share with their customers. At MA, the scientists were better equipped to discuss with their clients the full scope of their projects in order to launch them successfully and with fewer challenges down the road. Learning how to use questions to uncover important points earlier in the process was, as Wiley said, "a light bulb moment."

In learning how to ask the right questions at the right time—and how to better listen to the answers—they were able to discover more about their customers, uncovering those unknown unknowns that could lead to additional sales. This is very much in keeping with what we discussed in Chapter 5, in which we focused on the importance of discovering. In learning how to ask questions and listen to answers, the scientists/salespeople became better able to dig deep in order to expand relationships, accelerate the sales process, and close more deals.

It's also important to note that many of the scientists and sales reps at The McCrone Group were, in fact, already utilizing many Critical Selling skills, even though they at first didn't see it as such. At issue was the negative perception of how they viewed selling skills. The skills that were provided in the training were already being used—the mindset around those skills needed adjusting. In essence, some of the individuals involved in selling needed to accept the notion that a selling mindset wasn't a negative and that they could use Critical Selling skills to better educate customers and provide a better customer experience. In fact, the scientists were surprised to see that the selling skills Janek provided were things they were already doing and that if they perfected those skills they could improve the customer experience. Although at first reluctant to undergo sales training, they soon realized that they were all headed in the same direction, that they were using similar skills, and that they did in fact all want to better help their customers using improved selling skills.

The Results

Recall that The McCrone Group faced several challenges: the businesses needed to work together better in order to better coordinate customer needs; the organization as a whole needed to better leverage customer relationships; each business needed to be less reactive and more proactive in order to maximize sales; all of the staff needed to consider themselves not just scientists or technicians but also trusted advisors; and, finally, the organization needed to grow overall sales by reaching more customers and establishing deeper relationships.

Each of The McCrone Group businesses (MA, MMA, and HCAS) wanted to grow, even though they all went about it a little differently. Even so, all of the businesses experienced similar overall results, and one of the biggest of those positive results was the breaking down of silos as the entire staff started working more closely together in order to improve overall customer experience. In implementing the solution by preparing and planning, training the team, and sustaining the skills, Janek and The McCrone Group together effected two other primary results: increased sales and a shift in culture.

Increased Sales

As a result of the sales training, The McCrone Group has seen consistent year-over-year improvements in sales. In addition, the organization has seen more repeat customers, improved customer interactions, deeper reach into new markets, and more effective outbound sales efforts. The average deal size has increased because a more customer-focused approach has turned sales reps into trusted advisors, who are able to better identify needs and sell a broader array of products and services. As a result, trusted advisors enjoy richer customer relationships across the organization.

Bringing in Janek as an outside organization provided The McCrone Group with a more objective view of their situation. It allowed them to look at things differently. The training also provided the sales force with new strategies and tools to approach their customers, left the staff with a positive vibe, and had a direct effect on growing sales, which continue to increase year after year.

In the past, a customer would ask for a quote and a salesperson would provide it. It was a simple order-taking process. Leaders at The

McCrone Group recognized the need to grow. "We all wanted to grow," said McGinn. Opportunities would pop up time and again, and their scientists/salespeople would discuss issues with their clients, but there wasn't effective follow-up or management of customer relationships. "We realized that there was more here than what we were doing," says McGinn. "There are better ways to manage these relationships."

Since taking a customer-focused sales approach, The McCrone Group has been better able develop customer relationships. The training has resulted not only in increased sales but also in improved customer relationships—without sacrificing the technical and scientific expertise that the sales professionals at The McCrone Group needed in order to sell their products and services with confidence and authority.

"We're all salespeople now," says McGinn. "We love microscopy. We're scientists as well."

Culture Shift

The McCrone Group businesses experienced a shift in culture once they saw themselves as all part of one company, a whole team working together to connect with customers. In addition, everyone now sees that sales is an important aspect of what they do, which is better understanding customers' needs so they can tailor unique solutions to meet those needs.

As an organization, The McCrone Group today is better able to support their customers and to provide follow-up sales. When they started to ask the right questions of their customers, they were able to uncover new business in the form of future maintenance visits, qualification visits, and cross-selling opportunities. With their new skills in place, they were able not only to increase revenue but also to expand relationships, even at a time when their competitors were consolidating or merging. In short, they're all able to do their jobs better—and to do their jobs as trusted advisors in a way they weren't before.

"It's changed the culture," says McGinn. "It's changed our approach."

Leaders at The McCrone Group have seen a clear shift in their approach to selling, and their sales force has been effective at moving along The Relationship Continuum from order takers to trusted advisors. "It really has changed the mindset of the whole group," says Wiley. "Trying some of these things and feeling more confident asking questions made them realize that the part of the whole process that they were having difficulty with just took asking the right questions or using the right approach to make that not seem like it was the more difficult or bigger part of the project and allow them to focus on what they're good at and passionate about, and that's the science."

In the past few years, since undergoing sales training, The McCrone Group has seen some of their best business. Having learned how to ask the right questions at the right time has allowed the sales force to move into these new areas with aplomb, largely because they are more seasoned and more comfortable in working with customers to discover needs. The McCrone Group has seen new customers in new industries, increased revenues, larger projects, more repeat customers, and revived customers, not to mention happier staff members who are enjoying more success. In addition, the company has seen a motivational shift, with salespeople feeling more optimistic, enjoying stronger customer relationships, and knocking their sales figures out of the park. Since undergoing the training and putting their newfound skills to work, the scientists/salespeople at The McCrone Group have worked diligently to transform themselves from order takers to trusted advisors.

Notes

Chapter 1

1. Brent Adamson, Matthew Dixon, and Nicholas Toman, "Dismantling the Sales Machine," *Harvard Business Review*, November 2013. Retrieved from https://hbr.org/2013/11/dismantling-the-sales-machine.
2. Scott Gillum, "The Disappearing Sales Process," *Forbes*, January 7, 2013. Retrieved from www.forbes.com/sites/gyro/2013/01/07/the-disappearing-sales-process/.
3. David H. Maister and Charles H. Green, *The Trusted Advisor* (New York: Free Press, 2000).

Chapter 2

1. Emily Lawson and Colin Price, "The Psychology of Change Management," *McKinsey Quarterly*, June 2003. Retrieved from www.mckinsey.com/insights/organization/the_psychology_ of_change_management.
2. The Women's Initiative, "Report of the Steering Committee for the Women's Initiative at Duke University," August 2003. Retrieved from http://universitywomen.stanford.edu/reports/ WomensInitiativeReport.pdf. See also: Carol S. Dweck, *Mindset: The New Psychology of Success* (New York: Ballantine Books, 2006), 41.
3. Dweck, *Mindset*, 86.

4. Lawson and Price, "The Psychology of Change Management."
5. Ibid.
6. Gerhard Fischer, "Lifelong Learning: Changing Mindsets," Center for LifeLong Learning & Design (L3D), Department of Computer Science and Institute of Cognitive Science (Boulder, CO: University of Colorado), Undated. Retrieved December 10, 2014, from http://cphp.sph.unc.edu/lifelonglearning/toolkit/LLLChangingMindsets.pdf.
7. Ibid.

Chapter 3

1. Frank V. Cespedes, *Aligning Strategy and Sales: The Choices, Systems, and Behaviors That Drive Effective Selling* (Cambridge, MA: Harvard Business Review Press, 2014), 11.

Chapter 5

1. Susie Pryor and Avinash Malshe, "Listening, Empathy, and Sales Effectiveness," *Keller Center Research Report* 7, no. 3 (September 2014): 11–17. Retrieved from www.baylor.edu/business/kellercenter/doc.php/228744.pdf.
2. Lucette B. Comer and Tanya Drollinger, "Active Empathetic Listening and Selling Success: A Conceptual Framework," *Journal of Personal Selling & Sales Management* XIX, no. 1 (Winter 1999): 15–29.
3. Ibid.
4. Ibid.
5. Ibid.
6. Pryor and Malshe. "Listening, Empathy, and Sales Effectiveness."

Conclusion

1. Acuity Group, "2014 State of B2B Procurement Study: Uncovering the Shifting Landscape in B2B Commerce," October 28, 2014. Retrieved from www.acquitygroup.com/docs/default-source/Whitepapers/acquitygroup_2014-b2bstudy.pdf?sfvrsn=0.

2. Megan Heuer, "Three Myths of the '67 Percent' Statistic," *Sirius Decisions Intelligent Growth*, July 3, 2013. Retrieved from https://www.siriusdecisions.com/Blog/2013/Jul/Three-Myths-of-the-67-Percent-Statistic.aspx.
3. Lucette B. Comer and Tanya Drollinger, "Active Empathetic Listening and Selling Success: A Conceptual Framework," *Journal of Personal Selling & Sales Management* XIX, no. 1 (Winter 1999): 15–29.
4. *Ibid.*
5. *Ibid.*
6. Maria Vakola, "What's in There for Me? Individual Readiness to Change and the Perceived Impact of Organizational Change," *Leadership & Organization Development Journal* 35, no. 3, 195–209. Retrieved February 3, 2015, from http://dx.doi.org/10.1108/LODJ-05-2012-0064.

About Janek Performance Group

JANEK PERFORMANCE GROUP, headquartered in Las Vegas, Nevada, is an award-winning sales performance company offering sales training, sales consulting, and talent management services that drive real results. Janek works with a broad range of clients, from start-ups to Fortune 500 companies, in virtually every industry and vertical. Our solutions are tailored to meet the needs of the entire sales organization, top to bottom—from sales leaders and CEOs to the individual sales professional. Our team of sales experts is committed to staying at the forefront of what truly works in today's competitive sales marketplace. Our combination of ongoing research and real-world experience drives the development of our world-class sales training and perform- ance solutions. For more information on Janek Performance Group, please visit us online at www.Janek.com or call us at 800-979-0079.

About the Authors

Justin Zappulla

Managing Partner, Janek Performance Group

Justin Zappulla's career has been highlighted by remarkable performance in sales, sales management, and sales operations. Along the way, he has made a rapid climb from sales to corporate leadership positions and into sales performance consulting roles. Today, Justin, managing partner at Janek Performance Group, is considered one of the top authorities and thought leaders in corporate sales strategy and sales performance improvement.

Justin began his work at Janek Performance Group working face-to-face with a global clientele across a variety of industries and business segments, including technology, finance, insurance, health care, consumer goods, and manufacturing. With sales consulting, training, and coaching expertise, he has worked with hundreds of companies to develop and implement strategic sales performance solutions and has trained and coached more than 15,000 sales and sales management professionals worldwide.

Justin is an active member and supporter of several sales and learning communities, including the Association for Talent Development, and participates in both the Chief Learning Officer Business

Intelligence and Human Capital Executive Research Boards. Justin was a key contributor to the popular sales book *Mastering the World of Selling*, and as an often-quoted authority on sales and sales management practices, Justin has widely been recognized as one of the biggest names in sales.

Previously, Justin served as the international director of sales for the largest privately held telecommunications company in North America. In that role, he was responsible for B2B and B2C sales efforts and was a key player in launching and supporting the company's two international telesales centers, in Egypt and the Philippines.

Justin brings a drive and focus to everything he does, whether he's in the boardroom or on the golf course. A native of Las Vegas, Nevada, Justin lives with his wife, Megan, and two daughters, Alaina and Aubrey. Justin has deep connections to his community, which he has seen grow into one of the world's most vibrant cities.

Nick Kane

Managing Partner, Janek Performance Group

Nick Kane has maintained an escalating career in sales, sales management, and as a sales executive leading a variety of sales initiatives both domestically and abroad. Nick Kane serves as managing partner at Janek Performance Group, where is recognized as a thought leader and sales performance expert, guiding numerous organizations in improving their sales effectiveness. Prior to his role as managing partner, Nick served as senior vice president of Sales & Marketing at Janek, overseeing sales across all Janek offerings, including corporate sales training to a wide range of verticals, nationwide sales seminars, and sales strategy consulting. In that position, he was responsible for working with corporate clients to develop sales strategies and implement sales training programs. He also led efforts to expand Janek's training offerings, enhance service levels and client satisfaction, and cultivate a more client-focused environment, all of which are part of his current focus as well.

Previously, Nick served as director of national sales for the largest privately held telecommunications company in North America. In that role, he managed sales and marketing initiatives for business clients in the United States. In addition, he was involved in the development and implementation of sales training and performance improvement initiatives within the organization, which included cold-call outbound sales, inbound sales, large account management, customer service, and customer retention departments.

A member of the Association for Talent Development, Nick has trained more than 15,000 sales professionals worldwide during the course of his career, and he is passionate about helping sales professionals improve their selling careers—and, as a result, their lives.

A self-professed die-hard Lakers fan, Nick also enjoys a variety of other sports, as well as travel and automobiles. He is very involved in his community of Henderson, Nevada, where he has lived for more than 20 years.

Index